SENTIMENTAL JOURNEY:
Classic Greeting Card Poems For All Occasions

Say What You Feel—Quickly, Easily, Comfortably, with the Perfect Poem

JOANNA & KARL FUCHS

iUniverse, Inc.
New York   Bloomington

TERMS OF USE

Please read below for permitted uses. The purpose of this book is to add another layer of copyright protection, a quick, easy way to show copyright violators, and those who have authority over them, that these poems belong to Joanna and Karl Fuchs. For more details on *why* we need to restrict the use of our poems as detailed below, see www.poemsource.com/terms-of-use.html.

These poems were copyrighted as they were written, starting in 2005. They originally appeared on our Web site, www.poemsource.com, where additional poems are continually added. The Web site brings Joanna and Karl, a senior citizen couple, regular income, and all marketing efforts, including this book, are directed toward leading more visitors to the Web site.

Therefore, reproduction or use of any poem or poems must show, beneath each poem, both the author's name and the Web site address.

Permitted:
- Free personal, noncommercial use of the poems in this book on paper cards, or printed on sheets of paper (framed or not), given hand to hand or postal mailed or shipped to relatives and friends. The author's name and the Web site address must appear beneath each poem. It can be small print, just so it's readable.

- Free personal, noncommercial use of the poems in this book on e-cards, such as those available at Hallmark.com and other e-card sites. The author's name and the Web site address must appear beneath each poem. It can be small print, just so it's readable.

NOT permitted:
- Electronic delivery of any kind (except e-cards, with restrictions noted above), including, but not limited to e-mail, texting, messaging, etc. ***Please do not e-mail our poems.***

- Business or commercial uses of any kind, where the poems are sold, or affixed to items to be sold, or used to generate income, or to add any kind of value to a commercial enterprise, activity, event or publication, including Web and other electronic publications.

For additional details, or to request permissions not covered here, please contact us through the contact form at our Web site, www.poemsource.com. On rare occasions we allow the posting of ONE of our poems at a Web site or blog. Contact us to request permission.

Feel free to make small changes to personalize the poem for your purpose, i.e., "I" to "We," "she" to "he," "man" to "woman," etc.

Note that a final greeting at the end, such as "Happy Anniversary" Merry Christmas," "Get well soon," is appropriate. These have been omitted to save space.

CONTENTS

Anniversary Poems

General Anniversary Poems   x
Anniversary Love Poems   5
50th Anniversary Poems   11

Baby Poems

General Baby Poems   14
Baby Girl Poems   18
Baby Boy Poems   19
Baby Shower Poems   20
Baby Announcement Poem   21

Birthday Poems

General Birthday Poems   22
Daughter Birthday Poem   29
Brother Birthday Poem   30
Baby's First Birthday Poem   30
Fiftieth Birthday Poem   31
Birthday Love Poems   31
Father Birthday Poems   35
Funny Birthday Poems   38
Mother Birthday Poems   41

Christian Poems

General Christian Poems   46
Christian Easter Poems   55

Christmas Poems

General Christmas Poems   63
Funny Kid Christmas Poem   68
Teacher Christmas Poem   70
Christmas Love Poems   70
Christmas & New Year Poems   71
Soldier Christmas Poem   72
Christian Christmas Poems   73
Christmas Prayers   75

Holiday Poems

General End-Of-Year Holiday Poems   77

Father Poems

General Father Poems   80
Son to Father Poems   85
Daughter to Father Poems   86
Father's Day Poem From Wife   88
Stepfather Poem   89
Father-In-Law Poem   89
Grandfather Poems   90
Poem for Deceased Father   91
Christian Father's Day Poem   91
Father's Day Prayer   92

Friendship Poems

General Friendship Poems   94

Get Well Poems

General Get Well Poems   100
Funny Get Well Poems   105

Graduation Poems

General Graduation Poems   106
College Graduation Poem   110
Graduation Gift Thank You   110
Graduation Invitation   111
Preschool and Kindergarten Graduation Poems   111
Christian Graduation Poem   112
Graduation Songs   112
Graduation Prayer   115

Love Poems

General Love Poems   116
Teen Love Poems   128
Relationship Poems   129
Sad Love Poems   130
Short Love Poems   134

Mother Poems

General Mother Poems   136
Mother to Daughter Mother's Day Poem   142
Mother-In-Law Poem   142
Mother's Day Poems From Children   143
Grandma Mother's Day Poem   144
Wife Mother's Day Poem   144
Sister Mother's Day Poem   144
Aunt Mother's Day Poem   145
Friend Mother's Day Poem   145

Step Mother Poem 146
Mother's Day Songs 146
Memorial Mother Poem 147
Christian Mother's Day Poem 148
Mother Prayer 148

New Year Poems

General New Year Poems 150
New Year's Eve Party Poems 152
Happy New Year Song 153
New Year Toasts 154
New Year's Resolution Poems 156
New Year Prayer 158

Patriotic Poems

Veteran's Day Poems 159
Veteran's Day Prayer 162
Armed Forces Day Poem 162
Memorial Day Poems 163
Flag Day Poem 164
Fourth of July Poem 165
Soldier's Prayer 166
War Poems 166

Sympathy Poems

General Sympathy Poems 169
Pet Sympathy Poem 172

Teacher Poems

General Teacher Poems 173
Preschool and Kindergarten Teacher Poems 178
Poem From Teacher To Student 179
Sunday School Teacher Poem 179
Teacher Retirement Poems 181

Thanksgiving Poems

General Thanksgiving Poems 182
Kid Thanksgiving Poems 186
Funny Thanksgiving Poems 187
Thanksgiving Prayers 189
Thanksgiving Prayers for Kids 192

Thank You Poems

General Thank You Poems 193
Thank You for the Gift Poems 196
Thank You Pastor Poem 197

Valentine Poems

General Valentine Poems 198
Teacher Valentine Poem 203
Christian Valentine Poems 203
Family Valentine Poems 207
Daughter Valentine Poems 208
Son Valentine Poems 210
Sister Valentine Poems 211
Brother Valentine Poem 212
Mother Valentine Poems 212
Father Valentine Poem 214
Parents Valentine Poem 214
Grandparents Valentine Poems 214
Wife Valentine Poems 216
Husband Valentine Poems 219
Friend Valentine Poems 219
Funny Valentine Poems 224
Kid Valentine Poems 231
Valentine Love Poems 235

Wedding Poems

Wedding Card Poems 243
Wedding Invitation Poem 246
Wedding Program or Thank You Poem 246
Wedding Toasts 247
Wedding Vows 248

Miscellaneous Rhyming Poems

Spring Poem 251
Summer Poems 251
Fall Poems 252
Winter Poem 254
Miss You Poem 255
Retirement Poem 255
Thinking of You Poem 255
Inspirational and Life Poems 256
Forgiveness or Apology Poem 257

ANNIVERSARY POEMS

General Anniversary Poems

Anniversary Joy

Your anniversary is a time
For sharing your affection;
It's obvious the two of you
Have quite a deep connection!

We send glad congratulations
And heartfelt wishes, too,
For joyful happiness and love
In everything you do.

By Joanna Fuchs

Loving Pair

It takes two special people,
To make a loving pair;
There's a joy just being around you,
A feeling we love to share.

We send anniversary wishes,
For years of joy and pleasure;
May each year keep getting better,
With memories to treasure.

By Karl and Joanna Fuchs

Remember?

Remember the first flush of love
that drew you powerfully together?
It still feeds the unassailable bond
that makes your marriage so secure.
Remember all the qualities about each other
you found so endearing?
They are still there,

and new ones create sweet surprises.
Remember thinking that this love
would last forever?
Your love has strengthened and grown
into eternal affection and admiration.
Years from now, you'll look back
at this anniversary
and realize you love each other
more than ever.

By Joanna Fuchs

Anniversary Toast

Here's a toast to the two of you
As you celebrate together;
You're the poster kids for happiness,
In sunny or stormy weather.

Your love continues, warm and bright;
May it shine throughout the years;
You're an example for the rest of us,
So here's to you: Three cheers!

By Joanna Fuchs

Best Marriage

Your anniversary marks the day
When you both said "I do."
The two of you became as one,
A marriage bright and new.

Now time has passed; your love is strong;
You passed the early test.
Your tender bond grows with passing time;
Your marriage is the kind that's best!

By Joanna Fuchs

When You Found Each Other

When you two found each other,
you gained the finest prize:
a companion to share life's joys,
a friend who lightens burdens,
whose company is always a comfort.
When you found each other,
you embraced the love you had dreamed of,
the source of endless pleasure
and memories to treasure.
May your anniversary remind you
of how precious that day was,
when you found each other.

By Joanna Fuchs

Few So Lucky

There are few who are so lucky
To have the things you do,
Companionship and friendship,
And loving feelings, too.

As friends we wish these pleasures
Will last forevermore,
For we know that you will ever be
A couple whom we adore.

By Karl Fuchs

Love's Blessing

Life bestows love's blessing,
On a very special few.
And I believe it happened,
When life encountered you.

You are a perfect couple,
In a marriage that is blessed;
May your love shine like a beacon,
A guide for all the rest.

By Karl Fuchs

Favored Couple

No one can know what the outcome
Of spending years together will be.
Being happy together is a gift,
And enduring love is the key.

So here's to a favored couple;
Everything has worked right for you.
May your future bring more of the same,
And your love remain strong and true.

By Karl and Joanna Fuchs

Wedded Bliss

Another year for you in wedded bliss;
Did you guess it still would be as good as this?
Days filled with deepest friendship and affection,
A relationship of love close to perfection.

It's nice to know a perfect pair like you,
You prove a happy marriage can come true.
I hope with many more years you are blessed,
And each new anniversary is the best.

By Karl and Joanna Fuchs

Another Year

Another year to create
precious memories together;
Another year to discover
new things to enjoy about each other;
Another year to build
a life rich in love and laughter;
Another year to strengthen
a marriage that defines "forever."

By Joanna Fuchs

Let's Give A Cheer

Come everyone let's give a cheer,
In celebration of a couple dear,
A couple who in love unite,
Who are seldom cross and rarely fight.

To a couple who bring joy to all,
May you laugh and sing and have a ball.
May happiness surround you two,
That is what I wish for you.

By Karl Fuchs

Anniversary Wishes

May the good Lord see and bless you
On your anniversary day.
May He always be your companion,
And guide you on your way.

May your bonds of marriage strengthen,
Holding strong amidst all fears.
And may our friendship stay untarnished,
Through the wearing of the years.

By Karl Fuchs

Have a Bright And Happy Day!

Happy anniversary;
Have a bright and happy day.
Your marriage sets an example;
It shines in every way.

Through time your bond is strong;
It lasts through sun and storm;
You'll always have your love
To keep each other warm.

By Joanna Fuchs

Inspiration

You two are an inspiration to the world.
Looking at you, we know that
soul mates can find and keep each other,
commitment means something,
a great team can overcome life's troubles,
and love triumphs over all.

By Joanna Fuchs

Anniversary Love Poems

Deeply, Madly

Our wedding anniversary brings to mind
The happiness and joy you've brought to me,
Sweet memories--the laughter and the tears,
Devoted love you give abundantly.

The place I want to be is close to you;
There's ecstasy and peace in your embrace.
I know that I can cope with what life brings,
As long as I wake up to see your face.

You're all I ever wanted, and much more.
I look at you and I still get a thrill.
Our marriage is the best thing in my life;
I love you deeply, madly, and I always will.

By Joanna Fuchs

Each Year I Fall In Love Again With You

When I first met you all those years ago,
I fell in love so fast, I knew right then,
You were the one and only one for me;
I'd never have to look for love again.

Each anniversary finds us happier;
You are my light--my moon, my star, my sun.
You show me what real love is all about,
You fill my life with pleasure, joy and fun.

As time goes by, our love grows stronger still.
You're the most amazing man I ever knew.
I prize our anniversaries because
Each year I fall in love again with you.

By Joanna Fuchs

Anniversary Love Sonnet

You've always been the one I counted on,
Through joy and sorrow, laughter, and some tears;
You keep me grounded; you're my steady rock;
You're there for me through days and months and years.

Your sweet devotion never, ever fails,
No matter what I say or what I do.
Sometimes I wonder what I ever did
To deserve someone as wonderful as you.

I love you with a love I can't control;
I always want to be right by your side.
I want to touch you, kiss you and much more;
My passion for you cannot be denied.

Together we are satisfied and blessed;
Our marriage is the very, very best.

By Joanna Fuchs

Perfect Partner

All those years ago, my dear
You made my world complete;
You became my perfect partner in life,
And you've been a world-class treat!

We've loved and worked and made a home
That fills me with pleasure and pride,
And it's all because of the wonderful one
Who has lived through the years by my side.

Thank you my treasured and cherished love;
You've made my dreams come true.
Your loving and caring have made our marriage
A blissful adventure for two!

By Karl Fuchs

Our Love Still Grows

Our anniversary means a lot,
Much more than any another day;
I celebrate my love for you,
And cherish you in every way.

Through passing time, our love still grows,
A caring relationship to explore;
Our life together gets better and better,
And I keep on loving you more and more.

By Karl and Joanna Fuchs

Every Year

Every year that I'm with you
Has been better than before;
It's hard for me to even think
How I could love you more.

Every year you've graced my life
Has been full of happiness;
I love your caring face, your voice,
Your tender, sweet caress.

Every year when this day comes,
I'm filled with love and pleasure;
Happy Anniversary, Love,
My joy, my delight, my treasure.

By Joanna Fuchs

So Many Pleasures

When I was young, I couldn't think
What it would be like to be older.
How could I know it would bring such joy
Just to cuddle my head on your shoulder.

So many things bring happiness now,
Like a rub on the back, or a smile,
And my feelings for you are stronger today
Than they were when you walked down the aisle.

When I was young, my fondest wish
Was a marriage that could be this good.
Where we'd work through pain to laugh again
As loving partners should.

As the days drift by we're settling in,
To a life that's rich and rewarding.
Just sharing with you is a dream come true;
You're a pleasure well worth hoarding!

I'm happy with you; to me you just shine,
And I'm blessed and thankful that you are mine.

By Karl and Joanna Fuchs

Dear One

Dear one...that's what you are to me.
Years ago when we met, I fell in love with you.
Nothing has changed;
I love you still...more than ever.
When you're not near me, I feel an emptiness
I can't seem to fill.
When you are near, I feel complete.
I cherish your love and companionship
and always hope to please you.
I always wish for your happiness,
for I love to see the sparkle in your eyes.
I never imagined that someone could be
as important as you are to me.
Please stay near
and love me as I love you.

By Karl Fuchs

As Time Goes By

We are older now but better by far;
Who knows how good it can be;
Our love still grows like a plant in the sun
Or a wave rising up from the sea.

We laughed before, but we laugh more now;
Life is more fun so it seems.
Days are sunnier, the moon shines brighter;
Our life is the stuff of dreams.

We shared in the past, but today we share more.
There's a warmth that keeps growing inside;
We loved when we met; it was powerful then,
Yet now our love's strong as the tide.

You're the best, dearest thing to come into my life,
Like an angel from out of the sky.
And I know one thing sure: You'll be dearer still,
As time goes by.

By Karl Fuchs

Perfect Pairing

Dear one, for me we are the perfect pairing;
Every thought of you is filled with all my caring.
You're the real live answer to my fondest dreaming,
A perfect partner for a perfect teaming.

Each year I realize that it's all true;
I have the one I searched for, and it's you.
I'm lucky that I have you as my mate;
It's our anniversary; time to celebrate!

By Karl and Joanna Fuchs

Perfect Mate

After many years of trying
To be the perfect mate,
You've still keep up the effort,
And that's why you're so great.

My love for you keeps growing,
With each year that goes past;
The enjoyable times I spend with you
Are really quite a blast!

By Karl Fuchs

The Lake

The beauty of the lake is always changing,
With the light, the weather and the season.
Yet each change holds a splendor all its own,
Each viewing precious for its own reason.

In sunshine, golden stars dance across the water.
Moonlight shines a beacon in the peaceful night.
The wind causes whitecaps to erupt and roll,
While calm brings assorted reflections of light.

The water has a new costume each day,
Perhaps gray or green, aqua or blue.
Though each view is different, the lake is the lake,
Lovely in its every color, mood and hue.

My thoughts of the lake remind me of you,
My wonderful, loving partner in life.
Through sunny days and stormy times,
We've stayed together as husband and wife.

Your love is my beacon, my star and my light;
All your colors and moods are precious to me.
You make every day an enchanting delight,
And I'll love you for all eternity.

By Karl Fuchs

Half-Century Anniversary

A half century of marriage
Deserves a celebration;
Your 50-year relationship
Rates major acclamation!

Congratulations to you both
On your durable rapport;
Happy 50th anniversary,
And may you have many more!

By Joanna Fuchs

A Golden Couple

Half a century ago, they say,
A wonderful marriage began that day.
Two beautiful people joined as one,
And worked together to make living fun.

We celebrate now those fifty years;
We raise our glass and give three cheers:
To partners in life in both work and play,
It's our pleasure to share your golden day.

By Karl Fuchs

Nifty Fifty

Our family's full of joy because
You're celebrating your fiftieth;
And as your kids, we want to say
As parents, you're the "niftieth!"

On your golden anniversary,
We hope you have lots of fun.
We're happy for you, and for us, because
In the parent lottery, we won!

By Joanna Fuchs

Fifty Years

Fifty years is quite a while
For most good things to last;
But you're still together and still in love;
You must share a wonderful past.

We celebrate you this wonderful day,
And hope that your bond keeps on growing;
You're a pair we should study, and do what you say,
Because your secret is well worth the knowing!

By Karl and Joanna Fuchs

Continuing Joy

When something works well for 50 years,
There sure isn't cause for complaint;
Who can deny it's a remarkable feat?
(You'd think there'd be some, but there ain't.)

Congratulations to you on this special day;
Fifty years you've been loving and living;
Our wishes are for the continuing joy,
That your love and your marriage keep giving.

By Karl Fuchs

Smooth Sledding

We've admired you since your wedding;
We delight in the joy you've been spreading.
We know just where you're heading--
For nothing but more smooth sledding!

Of years, you've accumulated fifty;
We think that's really nifty!
With love, you're never thrifty;
You're really special, if you catch our drifty.

By Joanna Fuchs

Strong Union

It's your golden wedding anniversary,
And it makes me so happy to say,
Through the years I've gotten to know you well,
And I'm proud to applaud you today.

Now your union is golden; it's 50 years,
An accomplishment hard to achieve;
I hope you will flourish as more years go by,
And whatever you want, you receive.

By Karl Fuchs

Your Marriage Is Golden

A partnership like yours is rare;
50 years you've been together!
You've always been a loving team,
In sunny and stormy weather.

Nothing can tarnish your lasting love;
At 50 years, you're gold.
Your affection shines as you go through the years,
With each other to love and to hold.

By Joanna Fuchs

BABY POEMS

Time Well Spent

See tiny fingers and tiny toes,
Bright baby eyes, cute baby nose;
Hear baby gurgles and baby sighs,
As Mom and Dad sing lullabies.

Life is changed, but that's okay;
It's fun to spend glad hours each day,
Taking time for all the good
That comes along with parenthood.

By Joanna Fuchs

Cherish This Time

So your baby is here!
What joy and what pleasure!
Now your life is expanding,
To make room for this treasure.

A darling newcomer
To have and to hold--
Her smiles are more precious
Than silver or gold.

He'll demolish your schedule
Though he's helpless and small;
he'll make his needs known,
And he'll rule over all.

See, a new parent's work
Is just never quite done,
But you'll never mind,
'Cause it's all so much fun.

When you hear her cute giggle
You'll start "aahing" and "oohing,"

And she'll soon reply back
By "ga ga" and "goo gooing."

Those big innocent eyes
See a world strange and new;
To make sense of it all,
He'll look only to you.

So cherish this time
Of miraculous things--
The excitement and wonder
That a new baby brings.

By Joanna Fuchs

Your New Arrival

It's got a cute nose and big round eyes;
It's created excitement you can't disguise;
It's a wonderful baby from a perfect pair,
And that's reason enough for a great fanfare.

By Karl Fuchs

Dear And Special Treasure

A new family member has arrived,
Your darling, precious baby.
Your lives are filled with amazing love,
And sleep has become a "maybe!"

Congratulations! Now enjoy
Your dear and special treasure;
Your lives are better, now transformed
With childhood's awesome pleasure.

By Joanna Fuchs

A Baby Changes Things

A baby changes things;
They'll never be the same;
Your life is filled with wonder,
Since your little miracle came.

There's lots of things to do now,
But with the new tasks you face,
Your family gains more love,
And bonds time will never erase.

By Karl and Joanna Fuchs

Joy Without Measure

We heard the good news,
So it's hip, hip, hooray!
We're so happy for you,
And we hope and we pray
That your brand new addition
Is a wonderful treasure,
And along with the work,
He brings joy beyond measure.

By Karl and Joanna Fuchs

Treasured Offspring

As babies go, yours must be rare,
For it got its life from quite a pair!
No doubt your offspring is a special treasure;
It's from you two, and you're both a pleasure.

May he be a blessing and joy to you;
You'll be good parents in all you do.
We rejoice at this wonderful thing you've done;
Enjoy your baby and have great fun!

By Karl and Joanna Fuchs

Congratulations On Your Baby

We hear you've created a cute little tot;
You're staring adoringly; you love her a lot.
Congratulations! Good Work! Let's give a cheer!
You're baby will get cuter with every year!

By Karl and Joanna Fuchs

The Joy of Raising a Baby

We're glad you joined our family,
Yet some things make us wonder;
How can a little package like you
Have a voice that's loud as thunder?

You are so small, and oh so cute,
But you are never very shy,
For whenever you want something brought to you,
You just open your mouth and cry.

First you moved on hands and knees,
Then you were up on your feet.
We're chasing you all around the house;
We're tired; we need a retreat!

Your food is smeared on the table;
Your food is on the floor;
Seems the only place food didn't go,
Is in the baby we adore.

Diapers here and diapers there,
Stinky... smelly... Whew!
Diapers would have done us in,
If we didn't love you as we do.

We're glad you joined our family,
You're a unique and wonderful treasure.
So, despite the work of raising you,
Being your parents is a total pleasure!

By Karl and Joanna Fuchs

Collect Sweet Memories

We hear you have a new addition,
A sweet little gal who is quite a magician,
Transforming each normal adult who sees her
To a comical fool just trying to please her.

She'll wrap you around her little finger,
As around her crib you often linger,
Searching for what can make your hearts twirl--
The adorable smile of your baby girl.

Cherish each moment while she's still small;
Collect sweet memories for later recall,
For when she's grown up and on her own,
You'll wonder where the time has flown.

By Joanna Fuchs

Sweet Pink Angel

Congratulations on your new addition;
A baby girl is a treasure rare,
A sweet pink angel, a little doll;
Nothing else can quite compare.

Her smiles and coos will bring you joy;
She'll fill your hearts with love and pleasure;
So cherish these special infant times,
With your little girl, your precious treasure.

By Joanna Fuchs

A Natural High

What else could bring you so much joy
As the arrival of your baby boy!
His snuggly charms now capture you;
He's in your thoughts in all you do.

Nothing can fill you so full of glee
As bouncing your little boy on your knee.
His precious antics please mom and dad;
He's a bundle of blessings, this little lad!

His boyish grin enchants everyone;
He's just what you wanted--your boy, your son.
A baby boy is a natural high,
So have lots of fun with your little guy.

By Joanna Fuchs

Amazing Joy

There's lots of fun,
And we don't mean maybe,
Coming to you
With your boy baby.

Your life is filled
With amazing joy
By this adorable creature,
Your baby boy.

Watch him, love him,
Learn again how to play,
As your own inner child
Comes out more every day.

Take lots of time
To enjoy your son,
Because much too soon,
Childhood is done.

By Joanna Fuchs

Come to a Baby Shower

I'll soon be here to meet you!
I've got lots of fun to share,
And now here's a baby shower
To help my mom prepare.

So come and join the party,
With friends and family,
To anticipate the arrival
Of her baby--Hey, that's me!
[Sign it "Baby (last name)]

By Joanna Fuchs

Baby Shower Greeting

Your baby shower is here,
And I'm glad I got invited.
Here's a baby gift,
I hope you'll be delighted!

By Joanna Fuchs

Thank You for the Baby Gift

Thank you for the baby gift;
I know that I will use it.
I appreciate your thoughtfulness,
And the time you took to choose it!

By Joanna Fuchs

Thank You for the Present

Thank you for coming to my baby shower;
Thank you for the present.
That you were there is special to me;
Seeing you is always pleasant!

By Joanna Fuchs

Baby Announcement Poem

This is to inform you,
To keep you fully updated,
Someone's arrived at our house
To whom we are related.

He screams and then he wails
But he still brings us much joy,
For the arrival that we have
Is a brand new baby boy.

By Karl Fuchs

BIRTHDAY POEMS

General Birthday Poems

Another Year

I'm wishing you another year
Of laughter, joy and fun,
Surprises, love and happiness,
And when your birthday's done,

I hope you feel deep in your heart,
As your birthdays come and go,
How very much you mean to me,
More than you can know.

By Joanna Fuchs

Birthday Blessings

Instead of counting candles,
Or tallying the years,
Contemplate your blessings now,
As your birthday nears.

Consider special people
Who love you, and who care,
And others who've enriched your life,
Just by being there.

Think about the memories
Passing years can never mar,
Experiences great and small
That have made you who you are.

Another year is a happy gift,
So cut your cake, and say,
"Instead of counting birthdays,
I count blessings every day!"

By Joanna Fuchs

Birthday Happiness

As we observe your birthday now,
Your cake and gifts don't matter much.
These common things aren't really you,
Ribbons, paper hats and such.

We celebrate a person who
Brings happiness to everyone,
Someone who gives more than she gets,
And fills our lives with joy and fun.

So Happy Birthday, special one!
We hope you make it to a hundred and two,
Because we always want to have
The special pleasure of knowing you.

By Joanna Fuchs

Happy Birthday, Special Treasure

God gave a gift to the world when you were born—
a person who loves, who cares,
who sees a person's need and fills it,
who encourages and lifts people up,
who spends energy on others
rather than herself,
someone who touches each life she enters,
and makes a difference in the world,
because ripples of kindness flow outward
as each person you have touched, touches others.
Your birthday deserves to be a national holiday,
because you are a special treasure
for all you've done.
May the love you have shown to others
return to you, multiplied.
I wish you the happiest of birthdays,
and many, many more,
so that others have time to appreciate you
as much as I do.

By Joanna Fuchs

Perfect Birthday

On your birthday I wish you much pleasure and joy;
I hope all of your wishes come true.
May each hour and minute be filled with delight,
And your birthday be perfect for you!

By Joanna Fuchs

Happily Ever After

On your birthday, special one,
I wish that all your dreams come true.
May your day be filled with joy,
Wonderful gifts and goodies, too.

On your day I wish for you
Favorite people to embrace,
Loving smiles and caring looks
That earthly gifts cannot replace.

I wish you fine and simple pleasures.
I wish you many years of laughter.
I wish you all of life's best treasures.
I wish you happily ever after!

By Joanna Fuchs

Best Birthday

It's your birthday...
and I'm thinking how glad I am
that you were born.
You have given me so much--
supported me, encouraged me, cared for me;
I didn't even need to ask.
I celebrate your wonderful self!
I am in awe of your boundless generosity,
your infinite kindness--that gentle inner glow
that you so freely use to warm my life.
Your birthday is as much a celebration for me
as it is for you, maybe more,
and I wish for you the best of birthdays,
the best one ever.

May each birthday be better than the last.
Most of all, I hope you will always be
As happy as you have made me.

By Joanna Fuchs

Birthday Appreciation

Each year your birthday reminds me
That I really want to say,
I'm very glad I know you;
I think of you each day.

I hope you enjoy your birthday,
All the pleasures it has in store,
And because I appreciate you,
I hope you have many more!

By Joanna Fuchs

Happy Birthday Poem

Once a year I get the chance
To wish you birthday cheer.
It pleases me no end to say,
I wish you another great year.

So happy birthday to you,
From the bottom of my heart,
May your good times multiply
Till they're flying off the chart!

By Karl Fuchs

Birthday Wish

It's your birthday time again;
It's true; there's no denying,
Another year has come and gone;
You know that I'm not lying.

So for you, the birthday person,
Here's what I want to say:

I hope this birthday's the best one yet,
In every delightful way.

So happy birthday to you.
Have lots of birthday fun!
May your birthday wishes all come true,
Even if you have a ton.

By Karl Fuchs

You Are A Gift

Some people give the gift
of peace and tranquility
to every life they touch.
They are always who they really are.
They are blessedly reliable,
dependably good,
predictably pleasant,
loved and treasured
by all who know them.
You are one of those people.
You are a gift
of peace and tranquility
in my life.
Have a wonderful birthday;
You deserve it!

By Joanna Fuchs

Every Year On Your Birthday

Every year, on your birthday,
I think about how glad I am
that you were born,
how thankful I am
to have you in my life.
Every year is another year
filled with the special joys you bring
just by being yourself.
Every year, when you open your birthday gifts,
realize what a gift you are
to everyone who knows you,
especially me.

By Joanna Fuchs

Birthday Wishes For My Friend

On your birthday,
I wish for you the fulfillment
of all your fondest dreams.
I hope that for every candle on your cake
you get a wonderful surprise.
I wish for you that
whatever you want most in life,
it comes to you,
just the way you imagined it, or better.
I hope you get as much pleasure
from our friendship as I do.
I wish we were sisters,
so I could have known you
from the beginning.
I look forward to
enjoying our friendship
for many more of your birthdays.
I'm so glad you were born,
because you brighten my life
and fill it with joy.

By Joanna Fuchs

When Your Birthday Rolls Around

Because you mean so much to me,
I celebrate your birth.
Sharing time and space with you,
Rings my bell for all it's worth.

Whenever your birthday rolls around,
I contemplate once more,
How happy I am that you were born;
The thought makes my heart soar.

I wish your birthdays happened more,
So I could let you know,
How very much you mean to me,
And I could tell you so!

By Karl Fuchs

I Celebrate You

On your birthday, I celebrate you!
On your special day,
I'm thinking of all the wonderful things you are
that bring so much joy to others, including me!
I celebrate your unconquerable spirit,
that lets you meet every challenge
with confidence, enthusiasm and persistence.
I admire your sensitivity;
You see needs that cry out to be met
that no one else sees,
and you meet them,
out of your deep and caring heart,
out of your wisdom,
out of your strength.
I treasure your uniqueness;
There is no one else like you,
and I feel blessed to know
such an extraordinary person.
I appreciate you, respect you,
cherish you, look up to you.
Happy, happy birthday!
May each new birthday
be the best one ever for you;
You deserve it!

By Joanna Fuchs

Happy Celebration

Have a happy celebration,
One you'll always recall,
And be aware on this day of days,
You're the most special person of all!

By Karl Fuchs

Birthday Thanks

Another year has come and gone;
The sands of time keep trickling away.
Your birthday reminds me to let you know
I'm thankful for you each and every day.

By Karl Fuchs

Happy Birthday, Old Friend

Congratulations to you, my old friend,
Birthday wishes to you, I send.
You look good for your age, I could say,
But you look good to me any day.

When I look in the mirror, I sigh,
'Cause I know the mirror doesn't lie.
You're aging like me, so you see
You're getting to be an old guy.

By Karl Fuchs

Bright Joy

On your birthday,
I'm thinking about how much light and sparkle
you freely dispense wherever you go,
how your sunny smile lights up any gathering.
Every birthday marks another year
of you radiating positive, happy energy,
contagious happiness
that infects all who come in contact with you.
May your next birthday find you the same--
glowing from within,
beaming bright joy on everyone you meet.
I feel blessed to know you.

By Joanna Fuchs

Daughter Birthday Poem

For Daughter on Her Birthday

It's your birthday, but we got the gift...
a gentle, sweet, beautiful daughter
who is always a pleasure to be with.
You glow with sensitivity and compassion
generated from the depths
of your warm heart and kind soul.
A loving mom, a peacemaker,
a woman full of the joy of life,

that's you.
Anyone who spends time with you
is privileged to know
such an extraordinary person.
You are a great joy in our lives.
We love you, cherish you, treasure you
and wish that every one of your birthdays
will be the happiest yet.

By Joanna Fuchs

Brother Birthday Poem

Birthday Poem For Brother

I'm fortunate, and I'm glad
I got you for my brother;
Even if I had the chance,
I wouldn't pick another.

I'm happy you're in my life;
You're my winner, come what may.
May your birthday wishes come true
On your very special day.

By Joanna Fuchs

Baby's First Birthday Poem

Baby's First Birthday

It's your very first birthday, baby,
One candle on your cake;
Proud parents stare in wonder
At each new move you make.

We join in celebration,
As this special date arrives,
For baby has brought pleasure
Into all our lives.

We look forward now to seeing
How you progress and grow,
From the cute and tiny infant
You were one year ago.

So dig into your icing;
Enjoy your presents, too.
The reason for this day
Is a special person--you!

By Joanna Fuchs

Fiftieth Birthday Poem

The Big Five-Oh

So you are finally fifty;
Happy birthday on the big Five-Oh.
I guess you could fill a great big book
With everything you know.

A whole half century of living
Is nothing to sneeze about,
So if you're a little patched and worn,
Don't you dare frown or pout.

Ignore things that make you feel old;
It's really great to be fifty.
You're smart, attractive and good company,
And I still think you're nifty!

By Joanna Fuchs

Birthday Love Poems

I Love Just You

Hey, birthday love, I think of you
On days both dark and sunny.
You bring me joy in every thought,
My precious, loving honey!

So be my love for all our lives,
And I'll be your love, too;
Each birthday is another chance
To say, "I love just you!"

By Joanna Fuchs

A Birthday Sonnet For My Love

Another year has passed for you, sweetheart;
It's time to cut the cake and celebrate;
And once again, my love, I start to think
Of things about you I appreciate.

It means so much to have you in my life;
Your loving care fills up my days with pleasure.
Your warm and giving nature helps create
Close, special times together that I treasure.

I live within a safe and steady world,
Because you love me unconditionally.
Your easygoing ways mean that I'm blessed
With peace and joy and blissful harmony.

To me your birthday is a precious day;
I hope it brings you joy in every way.

By Joanna Fuchs

Another Birthday Together

Your birthday marks another year together;
Such happy times, I couldn't ask for more,
Spending precious minutes, hours and days
With you, my love, whom I cherish and adore.

We've shared so much, we two, in love and friendship;
Each year our bond just seems to grow and grow.
I always want to be right next to you;
To be with you means more than you can know.

You're always there for me with a loving smile;
I'm never happier than when I know you're near.
I thought my love for you could not grow stronger;
And yet I love you even more this year.

By Karl and Joanna Fuchs

I Got the Gift

It's your birthday,
but I'm the lucky man
who got to be with you for another year.
It's your birthday, and the older you get,
the more wonderful you become.

It's your birthday,
and I'm privileged to share the years with you.
It's your birthday, and each year
I find the depth of my love for you growing.

It's your birthday, and I look forward with joy
to each day we spend together.
It's your birthday, and I wonder how I got along
for all the birthdays I didn't know you.

It's your birthday, and it's amazing
how easy and enjoyable it is to be with you each day.
It's your birthday, and no matter what fate has in store for us,
I know it will be a pleasure to spend life with you.

It's your birthday, but I got the gift--
You in my life for another year.

By Karl Fuchs

Birthday Love

The special day that you were born
Is filled with many pleasures;
Our attraction and our caring bond
Are my life's greatest treasures.

Your birthday brings me happiness
And fills me with emotion;
My gift to you is all my love
And unshakeable devotion.

By Joanna Fuchs

More Than I Can Say

Your birthday fills me with happiness,
because being with you is my pleasure, my joy.
I'm hoping and praying for many more years,
many more birthdays
to reveal all the aspects of my love for you:
the warmth in my heart whenever you're near,
the ecstasy of being close to you,
the excitement of sharing our lives together,
the sweet peace of knowing you are mine.
On your birthday, be aware that
I love you more than I can say,
more than you can know.

By Joanna Fuchs

Happy Birthday My Love

My love, I wish you a happy birthday,
But it's me who has been blessed,
For I got to spend the year with you,
In our comfy, cozy nest.

You are a rare and beautiful person;
You have delightful attributes,
Like competence and intelligence,
And what's more, lots of cutes!

You have mental strength and character
To guide you on your way;
People sense this strength in you,
And care about what you say.

So let's celebrate your birthday,
Because without it I'd never have met
My darling, wonderful you,
The best thing that's happened to me yet!

By Karl Fuchs

Hoping You'll Get Older Birthday

You complain about aging,
yet every new sign that you're getting older
reminds me how blessed I am
to have you for another birthday, another year.
You worry about sags and bags and wrinkles
yet all I see
is the life and love in your eyes.
Your contagious smile still warms my heart;
Your silly humor still lifts me with laughter.
I hope and pray that you'll get older
and older and older,
because when you're 100,
I'll enjoy you and love you
even more than I do today.
Happy Birthday, Sweetheart,
And many, many, many more.

By Joanna Fuchs

Father Birthday Poems

Top-Notch Father

Not many can have a father
Who's half as great as you.
Others might try, but they fall shy
You're a top-notch father, it's true.

So that's why on your birthday,
I want to make sure you know,
I admire you sincerely and love you dearly,
And those feelings continue to grow.

By Karl and Joanna Fuchs

You Da Man!

Ever since my life began,
I realized that "You da man!"
I saw your wisdom, your courage too,
And I learned I could rely on you.

Your tolerant nature was really great;
Nevertheless, you'd not hesitate
To let me know when I'd been bad;
It must have been hard, but that's being a dad.

You're strong and smart and filled with love--
A gift to me from up above,
So here's a greeting from your biggest fan:
Happy Birthday, Dad, 'cause "You da man!"

By Karl Fuchs

We Celebrate Your Life

Of all the men in the whole wide world,
Whose praises are sung out loud,
There is no man whom I respect more,
Or of whom I am more proud.

Throughout the years you've worked so hard,
To provide us a happy life;
You've been there to help and give advice,
And you did it all without strife.

That is why on this day each year,
I pray all your wishes come true;
Today we celebrate your life,
So Dad, Happy Birthday to you.

By Karl and Joanna Fuchs

Good Man

Dad,
Every year, your birthday reminds me
how grateful I am that you are my father.
With all that's going on in the world today,
I'm thankful I get to watch you,
to look up to you, being an example of a good man.
What a privilege it is to observe your strength,
your competence, and your kindness.
I am so blessed to be under your wing,
your protection, your care,

learning important life lessons from you.
If all fathers were like you,
the world would be a very different
and much better place.
Happy Birthday, Dad,
from your admiring daughter.

By Joanna Fuchs

Real Father

Some fathers are just father figures;
A real father is still very rare;
That's why I value so highly
The father-son bond that we share.

I'm blessed to have a real father,
Who displays his love with such ease,
And that's why I say on your birthday,
I love you more than a mouse loves its cheese!

By Karl Fuchs

Best Dad

Happy birthday to the best dad I know,
A father I love and respect,
A dad who fulfills all his duties
To teach, to guide, to protect.

If everyone had such a father,
A really good dad like mine,
The world would be so much better,
It would look like God's own design.

By Joanna Fuchs

Milestone Birthday

I'm glad I got to keep you as my dad
For all these days and months and ninety years.
You've been a special father all that time,
And now it's time to give you ninety cheers!

Ten cheers for loving me no matter what;
Ten cheers to you for making me behave;
Ten cheers for always being proud of me;
Ten cheers for the encouragement you gave.

Ten cheers for all the fun things that we did;
Ten cheers for always coming home at night,
Ten cheers for teaching me so many things;
Ten cheers for making childhood a delight.

And now this birthday poem is almost through,
So ten cheers, Dad, just for being you!

By Joanna Fuchs

Funny Birthday Poems

A Birthday Workout

Hike across green Ireland;
Bike the USA;
Backpack through New Zealand,
But don't call it a day…

Do yoga in lovely Paris;
Jump rope in Katmandu;
Avoid Italian pasta,
(Well, maybe taste, but don't you chew!)

Climb atop Mt. Everest;
Do aerobics on China's Wall;
Lift weights on Mexican Beaches;
And honey, that's not all…

Shake your booty with native dances
In Fiji and Bora Bora;
Move your body and exercise
Like you've never done befora.

Okay; that's good; you're finished;
Now you can take a break;
You've finally burned enough calories
To have your birthday cake!

By Joanna Fuchs

Stop Fighting Me, and Oh Yeah, Happy Birthday

I'm old enough and therefore wise;
With age our brains grow bigger in size.
So I wish for you a long, long life,
So your brain can grow bigger and stop causing strife.

And although we often disagree,
There's a strong hope that I can see,
For it's birthday time; a year has passed;
Your brain is getting bigger fast.

Before too long, your bulb may light;
No longer will you want to fight,
Because when you have a brighter mind,
It will be easier for us to think in kind.

With each year you live your thinking grows stronger,
And that's why I wish you'll live a whole lot longer.

By Karl Fuchs

Birthday Reminder

It's your birthday, so don't feel down;
Don't think bad stuff and frown;
Your life should be filled with mirth;
Just look what you've done since your birth.

You started out really small,
Now you're really filled out and tall.
In the beginning you would just cry,
Now you can laugh if you try.

You've done quite well since your start,
So as you grow older take heart;
Keep up the good work and don't be a jerk;
Stay happy till you're an old fart.

By Karl Fuchs

Baby Power

Being born was great for me,
Though I can't recall the chore.
But every year I'm pleased to see,
That it's me they all adore.

My mom and dad stay close to me;
They claim to know me well;
They're proud to know a celebrity,
And me, I know they're swell.

They celebrate, they laugh and sing,
And gifts on me they shower;
I must have done a wondrous thing,
My birthday cries, BABY POWER!

By Karl Fuchs

Getting Older Birthday

It's birthday time again I see;
Another year's gone by.
We're older than we used to be;
The thought could make me cry.

For getting older is not such fun,
When there's hurting in your back,
And it's agony if you have to run,
And a pleasure to lie in the sack.

Yes, getting older is quite a bore,
But to not get old is worse.
So "Happy Birthday!" let's shout once more,
And to heck with our ride in the hearse!

By Karl Fuchs

Over The Hill At Forty

So it's your fortieth birthday;
Four decades have gone and passed.
They say when you get older,
Time goes twice as fast.

I wouldn't know, of course,
Since I am still quite young,
But for you, the music is over;
Your last song has been sung.

You're just over the hill at forty;
You went down without a fight;
Time rushes on, and soon
That "hill" will be out of sight!

By Joanna Fuchs

But Why?

On this day you blow the candles out;
On this day the gifts pile high;
For one day a year you're the special kid;
"This is really great," you sigh.
"One birthday a year is really fun;
I want two! I can't? But why?"

By Karl Fuchs

Mother Birthday Poems

I Celebrate Your Life

Mom, your birthday means so much to me,
To have you in my life another year,
The time I spent enfolded in your love,
Each day, each moment with you is so dear.

I cherish the very special bond we have.
You lift my spirit in so many ways.
I celebrate your life; I honor you,
And send to you my love and care and praise.

By Joanna Fuchs

Walking Sunshine

Dear Mother I love you and want you to know,
I think of you often wherever I go.
You lift me up; you're like walking sunshine;
I'm lucky to have a great mother like mine.

Your endless affection makes you special and rare;
I'm always amazed by how much you care.
What you've given to me I can never repay,
Thank you, Mom, on your special birthday.

By Joanna Fuchs

I Owe It All To Mother!

It's your birthday, Mom.
So I will raise a cheer.
Without you, my special, loving mom,
I would not be here.

Yes, I owe it all to you, Mom.
From the time that I was small,
You encouraged me in everything,
And tried not to let me fall.

Throughout my life your caring,
Brightened each and every minute.
You loved me and enriched my life,
And I'm glad to have you in it!

By Karl Fuchs

Great Mom

Happy birthday, Mom!
I hope everyone can see,
What a great mom you've always been,
And how much you mean to me.

I always think about you,
In times both good and bad,
For the things you taught are with me,
In happy times and sad.

On your birthday I wish you joy,
Just like you pass around.
May your good times multiply,
And happiness abound.

By Karl Fuchs

Cherished Mother

Every day since I was born,
My mother cared for me.
Now that's a lot of caring,
As anyone can see.

Please, Lord, protect my mother,
And keep her safe from harm,
For she is a cherished person,
With great wisdom, love and charm.

Lord, it's my mother's birthday
So please, help her to see
How much she means to us,
Her loving family.

By Karl Fuchs

A Mother Like I Want to Be

Each year I'm extra happy on your birthday;
Your day reminds me of God's gift to me--
A mom who gave her all to raise me right,
A mother like the one I want to be.

By Joanna Fuchs

The Most Special Day

Mom, Your birthday is
the most special day of the year,
because without you I wouldn't have
the all encompassing comfort
of a mother's unconditional love—

your love, for me.
You are always there for me, Mom.
Whenever I need you,
to cheer me up, make me smile,
bolster my confidence,
or sympathize with me and ease my worries,
you fill up my empty, hurting places
with your boundless affection.
Your loving presence in my life
gives me a reassuring feeling
of security and peace.
Thank you, Mom,
and Happy Birthday!

By Joanna Fuchs

Mother, The Best On Your Birthday

Mother, I wish you the best on your birthday;
No one has earned it like you.
You provide the love that makes our dream
Of a happy home come true.

Your family loves and reveres its Mom;
You enrich everything you come near;
You're our rock, our beacon and our pleasure,
And everything we all hold so dear.

By Karl Fuchs

To Mom from Her Pesky Kid

I really love my mother,
And it surely makes me proud,
To know I'm one of her pesky kids,
And to sing her praises loud.

My mother has a birthday,
Almost every year,
And on that day she'll ponder life,
And even shed a tear.

See, Ma don't like her birthdays;
She says they make her old,

But she's as sharp as she ever was,
If the truth be told.

My mother showed me lots of things,
About the world, you see,
So then I could teach my pesky kids,
The things my mom taught me.

By Karl Fuchs

CHRISTIAN POEMS

General Christian Poems

You're Always There for Me

When the world comes crashing in
And chaos rules my mind,
I turn my heart to you, Lord,
And pure, sweet peace I find.

You lift me out of trouble,
You comfort me in pain;
You nourish, heal and cleanse me,
Like cool, refreshing rain.

In times of joy and bliss,
When things are going right,
You lift me even higher,
And fill me with delight.

You listen to my prayers;
You hear my every plea;
I'm safe because I know
You're always there for me.

By Joanna Fuchs

To Do List From God

I ran my life in search of worldly things;
My time and will were firmly in control.
I thought I had no need for what God brings;
I gave no heed to murmurs from my soul.

"You're planning, doing all the time," it said,
"But something else is missing deep inside.
Your mind is whirling, but your heart is dead,
So turn to God and let go of your pride."

I did, and God said, "Here's My plan for you:
Give your life to Me, and just let go.

Have faith and pray, and read the Bible through,
And you'll have blessings more than you can know."

So simple, yet it brings me perfect peace,
Living life for God the way I should.
Direction, purpose, fullness and release—
Life with God is very, very good.

By Joanna Fuchs

We Need You, Lord

We need you, Lord.
Like lost wanderers in a burning, empty desert
thirst for cool, clean water,
we long for you to quench us.
In a world gone progressively mad,
with chaos all around us,
we seek refuge in the order and purpose of your law.
With evil sneaking, leaking everywhere,
spreading heavy darkness,
creating feelings of emptiness,
we hunger for your goodness and light.
Turn us around, Lord, we pray;
retrieve your sheep who have gone astray.
Draw us to the satisfaction
of your purity and righteousness.
Cleanse us, and make us more like you,
role models, examples, beacons,
for others who are searching for meaning for their lives.
Come, Lord Jesus.
We need you, Lord.

Matthew 5:16
Proverbs 4:18

By Joanna Fuchs

Just Like Me

Dear Lord, forgive our yielding to temptation;
Forgive our pride, our love of worldly things.
Have mercy on our love of sensual pleasure,
Compassion on the sins that self-love brings.

It must be hard to understand us sometimes;
So very different is your heart and mind.
But wait, I just remembered that you do know
What it's like to be a part of humankind.

You suffered just like we do, and you were tempted.
You lived with us so you could comprehend
The things that we go through each trying day,
So you could give us mercy, and be our friend.

Thank you for compassion and forgiveness;
Thank you for your love and empathy.
Thank you, Lord, for coming down from heaven
To experience life's trials, just like me.

By Joanna Fuchs

Save Me

Save me from myself, Lord;
Save me from my need
To always run my life, Lord,
To control my every deed.

Save me from my pride, Lord,
My focus on just me;
Help me learn to serve, Lord;
Show me how to be.

Save me from the world, Lord,
When tempting things entice;
Remind me of eternity
With You, in paradise.

I give my life to you, Lord
My every need you fill;
I'm resting in my faith, Lord;
You saved me, and you always will.

By Joanna Fuchs

Come To Jesus

Isn't there more to life?
Is this all there is?

Imprisoned by our need for control,
trapped by insatiable desires
for worldly pleasures,
we are oppressed by our desperate hunger
for approval and love, from everyone
except the One who loves us most.

Straining, fighting to release
a familiar yet unknown burden,
we struggle to flee the tension, the stress
from the inner knowing
that our lives are incomplete
without Him who created us.

Parched, thirsting for more, more, more
of something we can't even define,
racing in the wrong direction,
we search everywhere
except the one place
where what we really want
can actually be found.

Turn around.
Come to Jesus.
He is hope;
He is joy;
He is freedom,
direction, and purpose.

Come to Jesus.
Let Him carry your burdens.
Surrender your pain to His love.
Turn from darkness to the Son,
to the beacon Who will always light your way.

Come to Jesus.
He is waiting...
waiting to lead you home.

By Joanna Fuchs

Like You

Lord help me to be in Your holy will;
Tell me what to do today;
Lead me in Your righteousness;
Make me more like You, I pray.

Guard me against this corrupting world,
Its perverted priorities, temptations, too.
Direct my mind toward Your commands,
So I can focus my life on You.

Fill my heart with Your light and love,
So I can assist those I see in need;
With You as my role model, let me be
Like You in thought and word and deed.

By Joanna Fuchs

I'm Trying, But...

I'm trying, but...
what I want to do,
I don't do enough of,
and what I don't want to do,
I do too much of.
I know the rules for a Christian life,
according to the Bible,
and I'm trying; I really am, but...
heaven and eternity seem so far away,
and the rampantly materialistic world
presses in so close
from every direction, every side,
that I get distracted.
Focus, focus, focus!
I need to focus, laser-like
on a simple, God-centered life.
Do I really need
to make that frivolous purchase,
instead of giving the money
to someone who needs it
so much more than I do?
Can I watch that TV show,
read that book, listen to that song
that contains (and promotes!)

even a little bit of what the Bible forbids,
without being corrupted?
Do I do enough
to love and help and encourage others?
Pride always hovers, eagerly waiting
to subdue and conquer humility,
so I think too much of myself.
I know the rules;
the Bible makes everything clear.
Forgive me, Lord;
I'm trying, but…

Romans 7:15
Matthew 6:19
Matthew 22:39
Philippians 4:8

By Joanna Fuchs

Nothing We Can't Handle

No matter what distressing times I face,
When rain and storms replace the sunny weather,
When things I counted on fail to sustain me,
There's nothing we can't handle, Lord, together.

If those I thought were friends act more like foes,
If I start to lose the things I hold most dear,
I know that I can tell it all to You;
You want to listen to me and to hear.

When my earthly world dissolves before my eyes,
When problems seem too great for me to bear,
You'll always be there for me, Lord, I know;
I can come to you on bended knees in prayer.

It's such a comfort, Lord, to realize,
You'll always be my King, my Lord, my Friend;
To share my burdens, worries, and my cares,
You'll love me and support me to the end.

By Joanna Fuchs

More Like Jesus

Let us be more like Jesus
In everything we do;
Let's live a life of service,
A life that's fresh and new.

Let's relinquish worldly things,
And not be slaves to fashion;
Let's fill our hearts with love,
Forgiveness and compassion.

Yes, let's be more like Jesus,
Being always in God's will,
For if Jesus' light shines through us,
Our earthly purpose we'll fulfill.

By Joanna Fuchs

God in the Seasons

Lord,
In Spring we are reminded
of the magnificence of Your creation,
as the earth is covered in verdant green,
with splendid splashes of color,
and we witness birth everywhere,
of animals bearing their young,
of buds turning into leaves and flowers
and our own moods being reborn
with renewed energy and life.

Lord,
in Summer, we remember
the warmth of Your love for us
and the light of Your goodness.
Both are everywhere for those who look.
Thank You for butterflies,
birds and wildlife for us to enjoy,
water to swim in,
and weather that frees us to romp and play
while outdoor pleasures are at their peak.

Lord,
In Fall, we thank you for Your cooling breezes,
that bring relief from the relentless summer heat.

We see bright colors fading and dying,
leaves turning brown, crisp, disintegrating,
only to be reborn next year,
reminding us that every living thing, including us,
must die in some way before being reborn.

Lord,
In Winter, as white snow blankets the ground,
we are reminded of Your purity and Your perfection.
The complexity and beauty of each single snowflake
only hints at Your transcendent intelligence and creativity.
We hunker down and snuggle in,
knowing this season will wind down
and Spring will reappear, as it always has
because You created an orderly, predictable universe,
not by chance, but from your flawless design.

Thank You for the seasons, Lord,
and everything in them
that You created for our enjoyment.

By Joanna Fuchs

More Than Ever

In today's chaotic world,
With everything around us crumbling,
Morality held in contempt,
Our leaders false, corrupt, or bumbling,

More than ever, we need Christ
To lead us through this darkening place;
His absolute truth will light our way;
He'll lift us with His love and grace.

The Bible is our cornerstone;
In God's word, we take our stands;
Role models we will strive to be,
Examples of our Lord's commands.

Dear Lord Jesus, strengthen us
To complete the tasks you'd have us do;
We pray you'll lead us, guide us now
To know and love and follow you.

By Joanna Fuchs

Help Me Forgive

When rage and fury overwhelm my heart,
It's time to look to God's own Holy Word.
I search the Bible for His good advice;
My will to His commands must be deferred.

In Romans God reveals His love for me;
In all things God works only for my good;
He gives me blessings I can't understand;
I'd be peaceful if I'd do the things I should.

Jesus forgave so much; why then can't I?
I want to mold my life after His own.
I pray, I try, but my sinful nature wins;
Lord, help me, I can't do this thing alone.

In Colossians, I read about the peace of Christ;
Oh, how I long to feel it in my heart.
All I have to do is to forgive,
But Lord, it seems I don't know where to start.

I need to walk a mile in the other's shoes;
They're doing what they think they have to do.
I know some problems are blessings in disguise,
But Lord, sometimes I feel so doggone blue.

Ephesians says "Forgive as the Lord forgave you;
Get rid of anger and every form of malice."
I'd love to just let go and release it all,
But upon my heart is a wound that's become a callus.

I'll keep praying, trying, Lord, no matter what;
I'm determined to let go and relinquish blame;
Some day, I'll say, and be truly sincere:
"I forgive it all in Jesus' precious name."

(Romans 8:28, Colossians 3:13, Ephesians 4:31)

By Joanna Fuchs

Easter Joy

Jesus came to earth,
To show us how to live,
How to put others first,
How to love and how to give.

Then He set about His work,
That God sent Him to do;
He took our punishment on Himself;
He made us clean and new.

He could have saved Himself,
Calling angels from above,
But He chose to pay our price for sin;
He paid it out of love.

Our Lord died on Good Friday,
But the cross did not destroy
His resurrection on Easter morn
That fills our hearts with joy.

Now we know our earthly death,
Like His, is just a rest.
We'll be forever with Him
In heaven, where life is best.

So we live our lives for Jesus,
Think of Him in all we do.
Thank you Savior; Thank you Lord.
Help us love like you!

By Joanna Fuchs

Easter Means Eternal Life

A perfect God demands a perfect justice;
He cannot let us get away with sin.
We used God's gift of our free will to trespass,
So heaven's gates were closed; we couldn't get in.

Our sin required our blood, a sacrifice,
To atone for all the wrongs that we had done.
"But I love them!" cried our Father, filled with sorrow;
"I'll send my only Son to be the one."

Good Friday marks the slaying of our Jesus,
The unblemished lamb, the perfect sacrifice.
He took our guilt and blame upon Himself,
So we could be with Him in paradise.

On Easter morning, he came back from death;
He vanished from the tomb, the empty grave.
His resurrection means eternal life
For us, the ones he came to earth to save.

This summarizes all the Easter story
And because of it, we'll be with Him in glory.

By Joanna Fuchs

His Love

God sent His Son to take the punishment
For all the thoughtless, sinful things we do;
Jesus gave his life because He loves us;
His love is boundless, sweet, forever true.

On Easter morn He showed He is our Savior;
His resurrection proves He is our Lord.
That is why we tell you, "Happy Easter!"
He secured our heavenly reward!

By Joanna Fuchs

Without Easter

Without Easter,
there would be no hope of heaven.
Without the hope of heaven,
there would be no repentance,
no personal transformation,
no attempt to follow biblical principles.
Without Easter,
the world would be in chaos

and darkness.
Jesus' death and resurrection
means we can be reborn,
to live better, to do better,
to shine light into the shadows.
Hallelujah!
Happy, Happy Easter.

By Joanna Fuchs

Celebrate Our Savior

On Easter morn, we celebrate our Savior;
Whatever people seek in Him, they find.
In history, there has never been another
So holy, sacrificial, good and kind.

His resurrection makes us all immortal;
In heaven, we'll be together with our King.
Eternally we'll share in all His blessings;
Happy Easter! Jesus Christ is everything!

By Joanna Fuchs

He Lives

Happy Easter! Hallelujah!
Jesus Christ, He lives!
Serve Him to receive salvation;
Eternal life he gives!

By Joanna Fuchs

A Second Chance

God always wants the best for us,
But in Eden we sinned; we really blew it.
We disobeyed God's direct decree;
We separated from Him, and we knew it.

You'd think we'd learn to behave ourselves,
But through all time, we just kept doing it;

Piling wrong on top of wrong,
Our punishment—we kept accruing it.

Jesus came and changed all that;
He paid the price for all our sins;
When we repent and believe in Him,
We change, and a better life begins.

Easter stands for a second chance
For us to choose to put things right;
If we repent, and really believe,
Our record is polished clean and bright.

When Jesus rose from the dead back then,
He guaranteed our eternal life,
Reunited with God in heaven,
Free from tears and fears and strife.

Easter ensures paradise
For all of us, for you and me;
We're reconciled to our Lord and King
For now and all eternity.

By Joanna Fuchs

If Not For Easter

If not for Easter,
the chaos of this world
would be all there is
and all there ever would be.
If not for Easter,
the unfairness of life
would drive us to despair.
But God sent His Son
to give eternal life
filled with peace, happiness
and unimaginable blessings
to those who choose Him.
All we have to do is choose Him.
Happy, Happy Easter!

By Joanna Fuchs

The Easter Story

Jesus came to compensate
For all the wrongs we do.
He came to earth to die for us,
So we'd be born anew.

"This bitter cup, let it pass from me,"
He cried, in a plaintive voice;
"Yet not My will, but Thine be done;"
He said, in His faithful choice.

The Judas kiss would seal his fate;
He faced a hostile crowd;
The governor, Pilate, saw through it all;
Jesus' guilt he disavowed.

"I wash my hands of all of this,"
Said Pilate, "Let Him be."
But the crowd yelled "Crucify him now,
And set Barabbas free!"

Pilate yielded to their wish;
And Jesus was led away.
The soldiers beat him, and mocked Him, too,
Yet He continued to obey.

A crown of thorns lay on His head,
As His sentence was carried out;
His hands and feet were pierced with nails,
But He did not scream or shout.

"Father, forgive them for this crime;
They know not what they do."
He said this despite His torment, because,
He was thinking of me and you.

"It is finished," he sighed in His anguish and pain,
As His body gave up to death.
The curtain tore, and darkness fell,
After He took His last breath.

The best of the story is the very last part;
It's why on Easter we're filled with pleasure:

Death could not our Savior hold;
His power is beyond all measure.

He rose from the grave, and was seen all around;
Ever since, He's inspired devotion,
And we'll be with Him for eternity,
When we get our heavenly promotion.

That's why Easter is a major event:
He suffered and died in our place.
He rose and forgave us and loves us still,
Our Savior of matchless grace.

By Joanna Fuchs

Jesus Loves Me; Easter Tells Me So

(To Be Sung to the Tune of "Jesus Loves Me)

Jesus loves me, this I know;
The Easter story tells me so.
He died for me to bear my sin;
He opened heaven to let me in.

Yes, Jesus loves me;
Yes Jesus loves me;
Yes Jesus loves me;
Easter tells me so.

Jesus loved me when He died,
Loved me enough to be crucified.
But His death didn't last very long,
Because His power is so strong.

Yes, Jesus loves me;
Yes Jesus loves me;
Yes Jesus loves me;
Easter tells me so.

Jesus' came back from the dead
I know because the Bible said.
Jesus is my Lord and King;
Love and praise to Him I bring.

Yes, Jesus loves me;
Yes Jesus loves me;
Yes Jesus loves me;
Easter tells me so.

When I die, I'll rise up, too.
We'll all be in heaven, me and you.
We'll see Jesus face to face.
Up in heaven, that happy place.

Yes, Jesus loves me;
Yes Jesus loves me;
Yes Jesus loves me;
Easter tells me so.

The Easter story brings much joy
To us all, each girl and boy.
Jesus is my Savior now;
Heaven and earth to Him must bow.

Yes, Jesus loves me;
Yes Jesus loves me;
Yes Jesus loves me;
Easter tells me so.

By Joanna Fuchs

What Easter Means to Me

(To Be Sung to the Tune of "Michael, Row the Boat Ashore)

Easter morning, God be praised,
Allelujah!
Jesus Christ from death was raised.
Allelujah.

On Good Friday, Jesus died;
Allelujah!
All for us, He was crucified.
Allelujah.

Jesus bore the pain for me,
Allelujah!
From my sin, to set me free.
Allelujah.

Death could not confine our Lord,
Allelujah!
And to life He was restored.
Allelujah.

Easter morn we consecrate,
Allelujah!
His resurrection to celebrate.
Allelujah.

Jesus' love means when we die,
Allelujah!
We'll live in heaven with Him on high.
Allelujah.

Our Savior loves us awesomely;
Allelujah!
That's what Easter means to me.
Allelujah.

By Joanna Fuchs

CHRISTMAS POEMS

General Christmas Poems

The Christmas Gift of Knowing You

The Christmas season fills our hearts with joy;
Bright, happy days bring special kinds of pleasure.
We're wrapped in the excitement of it all,
The sights, the sounds, the smells, the tastes we treasure.

Yet when we have some quiet time to think
About our finest blessings all year through,
We focus on our family and our friends,
And appreciate the gift of knowing you!

By Joanna Fuchs

Christmas Joys

Evergreen boughs that fill our homes
With fragrant Christmas scents,
Hearts filled with the loving glow
That Christmas represents;

Christmas cookies, turkeys stuffed,
Festive holly berry,
Little faces bright with joy,
Loved ones being merry;

Parties, songs, beribboned gifts,
Silver bells that tinkle,
Christmas trees and ornaments,
Colorful lights that twinkle;

Relatives waiting with open arms
To smile and hug and kiss us;
These are some of the special joys
That come along with Christmas.

By Joanna Fuchs

What Do We Love About Christmas?

What do we love about Christmas;
Does our delight reside in things?
Or are the feelings in our hearts
The real gift that Christmas brings.

It's seeing those we love,
And sending Christmas cards, too,
Appreciating people who bring us joy
Special people just like you.

By Joanna Fuchs

Recipe for Christmas All Year Long

Take a heap of child-like wonder
That opens up our eyes
To the unexpected gifts in life—
Each day a sweet surprise.

Mix in fond appreciation
For the people whom we know;
Like festive Christmas candles,
Each one has a special glow.

Add some giggles and some laughter,
A dash of Christmas food,
(Amazing how a piece of pie
Improves our attitude!)

Stir it all with human kindness;
Wrap it up in love and peace,
Decorate with optimism, and
Our joy will never cease.

If we use this healthy recipe,
We know we will remember
To be in the Christmas spirit,
Even when it's not December.

By Joanna Fuchs

The Nicest Present

Under the tree the gifts enthrall,
But the nicest present of them all
Is filling our thoughts with those who care,
Wanting our Christmas joy to share.

To you, whom we're often thinking of,
We send our holiday joy and love.

By Joanna and Karl Fuchs

Christmas Magic

Are we too grownup to feel a thrill
As we light the Christmas tree?
Are we immune to cookies,
Christmas cards and Christmas glee?

Are we too adult to "Ooh" and "Aah"
At the Christmas candle's glow?
Are we blasé about our gifts;
Do we shun the mistletoe?

Are we too mature for carols,
For merry or for jolly?
Do the decorations leave us cold,
The ornaments and holly?

Fat chance! We'll never grow too old
To love the Christmas magic.
A year without a Christmas
Would be boring, even tragic.

So bring it on! The candy canes,
The feasting and good cheer;
O Christmas, lovely Christmas,
You're the highlight of the year!

By Joanna Fuchs

Christmas Fun

The tempting gifts are tantalizing;
About opening them, we are fantasizing.
The holiday foods are appetizing;
Our excitement and joy are growing and rising;
Our hearts and minds are harmonizing;
Jolly Christmas fun we're maximizing!

By Joanna Fuchs

Family Joys

Christmas is filled with special joys,
And the very best of all
Is contemplating those dear to us,
And the memories we recall.

We often think at Christmas time
Of people, affectionately,
And we realize how blessed we are
To have you in our family.

By Joanna Fuchs

Year-Round Joy

Christmas is full of shiny things
That sparkle, gleam and glow;
These holiday pleasures dazzle us,
And yet, deep down, we know...

That Christmas has its special gifts,
But our year-round joy depends
On the cherished people in our lives,
Our family and our friends.

By Joanna Fuchs

Holiday Feasting

Holiday time is for feasting;
We look forward to each treat.

The tables are full of our favorite foods;
We've got lots of good things to eat.

We scarf marshmallowed sweet potatoes;
There's cider and eggnog to slurp.
There's so much going down at once,
Who can help an occasional burp?

Here's the turkey, dressing and gravy;
Let's all get down to chewing it,
And if we pass a little gas,
Who'll notice? Everyone's doing it.

Dessert is three kinds of pie;
Then pass the box of candy.
Next year will you please remind us
To have Alka-Seltzer handy!

By Joanna Fuchs

This Christmas

We hope this Christmas enriches your life;
May each day be happy and bright,
Overflowing with pleasure and love;
May your Christmas be filled with delight.

By Karl Fuchs

Memories To Treasure

May the days until Christmas be full of sweet pleasure,
And your holidays create joyful memories to treasure.

By Joanna Fuchs

A Sunny Christmas

Every year at Christmas time
There's not a sign of snow.
Instead we spend our yuletide days
In the sun's warm cheery glow.

We have the best of Christmas things,
The lights, the gifts, the bells,
(And "snowbirds" who arrive en masse
To fill our beach hotels.)

The glorious weather fits right in
With our happy Christmas mood,
And we can also walk and run
Without having to be snow shoed.

So don't feel bad for your Florida friends
Who have no snow or ice.
We think our sunny Christmas here
Is a holiday paradise!

By Joanna Fuchs

My Christmas Wish For You

Christmas trees, presents and holly wreaths,
The feeling of love, like a warm embrace,
Family and friends surrounding you,
With Christmas joy in each precious face.

By Joanna and Karl Fuchs

Funny Kid Christmas Poem

Toy Escape

Late Christmas Eve, when all was still,
And the room was dark as night,
The Christmas tree lit magically;
It was a fantastic sight!

Then from around the tree trunk came,
A strange and funny sound,
As gifts began to unwrap themselves,
And toys jumped out all around.

The music box began to play,
And in a crazy trance,

The candy canes jumped off the tree
To do a silly dance.

The big stuffed bear leaped to his feet,
To see what he could see;
He rode a shiny, bright red bike
Around the Christmas tree.

The new toy kitchen started to cook,
And before you could blink an eye,
The oven door opened, and from inside
Came a tiny pizza pie.

A squirt gun squirted everything;
It knew what it was for;
By the time that it was emptied out,
A big puddle lay on the floor.

A beautiful doll with golden hair
Was searching for a friend;
A toy soldier marched up and took her hand;
They were a perfect blend.

In the bedroom were a boy and girl,
Asleep in Christmas dreams;
The soldier saluted; the doll gave a kiss;
At least that's the way it seems.

Now everything began to tire;
The toys went back in place,
But when mother woke in the morning,
You should have seen her face.

The tree was fine; the gifts were there,
Yet mother gave a roar;
She looked at her wet shoes and yelled,
"What's this puddle on my floor?"

By Joanna Fuchs

Teacher Christmas Poem

For My Teacher At Christmas

Christmas vacation is great;
My time is mine to spend;
I can be with friends or watch TV;
I wish it would never end.

I don't miss school or homework;
I really like to be free;
But I'll miss you when I'm gone from school;
You're just what a teacher should be.

So have a perfect Christmas;
Be sure to have lots of fun;
I look forward to seeing you again,
When Christmas vacation is done.

By Joanna Fuchs

Christmas Love Poems

Christmas Love

At Christmastime I think of all the gifts
That bring me great delight and sweet surprise,
But nothing in this world can bring such joy
As you do, when you look into my eyes.

And when I contemplate what Christmas means,
The caring and the giving--I confess,
You've given me the things I want the most:
Your love, your touch, your kiss, your warm caress.

The Christmas tree reminds me, with its lights
That just the thought of you sets me aglow;
You light me up from deep within my heart,
Because I cherish you, and love you so.

With you it's Christmas all the time, sweetheart.
I treasure every hour and every minute.

Your love is all I'll ever want because,
My life is so fulfilling with you in it.

By Joanna Fuchs

Be My Christmas Gift

If you sat beneath the Christmas tree,
You'd sure add to the décor,
But even if you were gift wrapped, dear,
I couldn't love you more.

You have to know that if I had you,
I'd have the gift I'd most adore,
Better than any expensive gift
I could purchase in a store.

If you hug me tight, you wonderful thing,
And be my Christmas gift,
You'll brighten my days forevermore
And give my heart a lift.

By Karl Fuchs

Christmas & New Year Poems

Christmas New Year Wish

I made a Christmas wish for you,
For a holiday full of pleasure,
Friends and family all around,
And memories to treasure.

I wish for you a Christmas filled
With joyous holiday cheer;
I wish you a Merry Christmas,
And a very Happy New Year!

By Joanna Fuchs

Merry Christmas and Happy New Year

We're wishing you a Christmas
Full of laughter, love and light,
With delicious holiday foods
To excite your appetite.

We're hoping you receive
Delightful gifts to make you smile,
With family and friends
To love you all the while.

We wish you a Merry Christmas;
May your Christmas dreams come true,
And when Christmas is over,
Happy New Year, too!

By Joanna Fuchs

Soldier Christmas Poem

A Soldier Is A Gift

As we celebrate Christmas, and we open our gifts,
we realize what priceless gifts a soldier gives to our country—
gifts of patriotism, service, and deep dedication to our nation.

As we feast on a variety of fine Christmas delicacies,
we acknowledge that a soldier personifies a variety of fine qualities:
courage, good character, honor, fortitude amidst hardship,
persistence in subduing evil, and bravery in the face of danger.

A soldier is a cut above the rest of us,
doing jobs we could not or would not do.
While we are surrounded by Christmas comforts,
we remember soldiers in places we would not want to be,
bringing the gift of adaptability to any situation,
no matter how harsh or difficult.

As we "ooh" and "aah" over the Christmas lights and shiny ornaments
we recognize that a soldier gives us the most cherished gift of all,
the shining light of freedom.

At Christmas, let us wrap our hearts and minds
around our treasured soldiers.
May they understand how very much their service means to us.
Let us send the Christmas gifts of love, respect and admiration
to our steadfast, loyal, magnificent warriors
and their essential civilian support staff.

They themselves are the most precious Christmas gift of all,
our protectors—our soldiers.

By Joanna Fuchs

Christian Christmas Poems

A Different Kind Of Christmas

Sometimes Christmas is just overwhelming, it seems,
As we rush around buying up stuff.
We spend without end, and we rack up those bills,
But it feels like it's never enough.

So this Christmas, let's all take a different approach:
Let's try to be more in accord
With God's Christmas gift, the best one of all--
Our sweet Jesus, our Savior, our Lord.

We'll be gentle and patient, and loving and kind,
And we'll keep our priorities straight;
The gifts of the Spirit, the gifts of the heart
Are the ones that we'll all celebrate.

And our stress will decrease, and we'll feel more at peace,
As we decorate, package, and trim;
Our new Christmas will be a pure joy and delight,
As we try to be much more like Him.

By Joanna Fuchs

True Christian Christmas

Christmas isn't showy gifts
Or glittering decoration;
It's honoring our Savior, Jesus Christ
In humble adoration.

It's serving those less fortunate,
Meeting their needs before our own;
It's making sure at Christmas time
That no one is alone.

It's taking what we would have spent
On things that no one needs,
And using it to help someone
With service and good deeds.

Our Savior showed us how to live
With charity, faith and service.
It makes the holidays a joy,
More peaceful, and less nervous.

So let's remember Christmas is
About our Savior's birth;
That's the way to genuine happiness,
The way to peace on earth.

By Joanna Fuchs

The Real Reason

Excitement and joy are filling the air;
The lights add special decor.
We're shopping for presents everywhere,
But are gifts what Christmas is for?

The wreaths and the trees and the parties
Aren't what we need to convey;
It's the birth of our Savior, Jesus,
The real reason for this holiday.

By Karl and Joanna Fuchs

Jesus Is The Reason

In Bethlehem, God gave to us
The source of Christmas joy;
A star shown on a miracle:
The virgin birth of a boy.

Jesus was born both God and man,
A Savior for us all,
The way to get to our heavenly home,
If we just heed His call.

So as we shop and spend and wrap
And enjoy the Christmas season,
Let's keep in mind the sacred truth:
Jesus is the reason.

By Joanna Fuchs

Christmas Prayers

Christmas Treasure

Dear Lord, we're here at Christmas time
To honor your sacred birth,
Dear Savior, thank you for bringing all
Your precious gifts to earth.

As we delight in this holiday
With its bright and special pleasure,
We pray to remember all year round
That You are the only true treasure.

By Joanna Fuchs

Christmas Blessing

Dear Lord,
We thank You for being here with us
as we celebrate this cherished holiday
to honor Your precious, sacred birth.
We recognize and acknowledge
that all the material pleasures we enjoy today,
the food, the gifts, and everything else
come from You, Lord,
through your grace, your compassion,
and Your love for us.
Help us throughout the year
to always strive to be worthy
of all the blessings You have given us,

our family, our friends and our comforts,
by living our lives in Your will
according to Your Holy Word.
We pray that You will bless this food
and everyone at this table.
In Jesus' name we pray, Amen.

By Joanna Fuchs

We Celebrate Your Birth

Dear Lord, as we celebrate Your birth,
let us remember that You are the true reason for Christmas.
Let every sparkling light remind us how You illuminate our lives,
a shining beacon to guide us in our thoughts and actions each day,
and how You light us from within
in the knowledge of Your love and truth.
Let the Christmas trees, standing straight, tall, unbowed,
remind us of Your uprightness, Your goodness, Your perfection,
and Your refusal to bow to worldly temptations,
no matter how great the challenge or trouble.
Lord, as we feast on Christmas treats,
let us remember that You are the sole provider
of everything worth having, that all good things come from You.
And as we enjoy our gifts, let us never forget
that You are the greatest gift of all--our wonderful Savior,
Counselor, Giver of an eternal life whose wonders we cannot imagine.
So as we delight in Christmas, the happiest and brightest of holidays,
let us remember there would be no Christmas without You, Lord,
and let us our hearts be filled with joy, and love
and thankfulness, this Christmas and all the ones to come.

By Joanna Fuchs

HOLIDAY POEMS

General End-Of-Year Holiday Poems

Those Who Are Dear

The turkey's bought and will soon be stuffed;
The guest room's ready, the pillows fluffed.
The closet's full of holiday gifts;
The snow is here, piled up in drifts.

Our plans are made for the coming New Year;
It's time to contemplate those who are dear.
We're thinking of you and how special you are;
Next to your name, we've put a star.

"Why?" you ask; well here's a clue:
We feel so blessed that we know you.

By Joanna Fuchs

Holiday Wishes

We wish for you a holiday
That's better than your dreams,
Filled with peace, good will and hope
And firelight that gleams,

Overflowing with holiday spirit
Good food and holiday laughter;
And when it's done, we hope that you
Live happily ever after!

By Joanna Fuchs

Special Holidays

We're thinking of you this time of year,
Wishing you happiness, joy, and cheer.
May all your days be warm and bright,
And your nights enhanced by holiday light.

Enjoy your delectable holiday foods,
As parties and gifts create holiday moods.
Favorite people play a meaningful part,
While treasured rituals warm your heart.

You are special to us in many ways,
So we wish you Happy Holidays!

By Joanna Fuchs

That Time Of Year

That time of year's come 'round again,
So we wish you all the best.
The joy that comes from knowing you
Makes us feel that we've been blessed.

So we'll share with you our feelings
At this special time of year:
May your holidays be a delight,
Filled with happiness and cheer.

By Karl and Joanna Fuchs

Bright Happy Time

The end-of-year holidays are here at last,
That bright, happy time when we have a blast!
Our wish when your new year has finally begun:
That you look back at months full of pleasure and fun.

By Joanna Fuchs

Joyful Holiday

At this sparkling, joyful time of year,
We think of people who are special and dear;
We're sending this poem in the hopes it conveys
Our best wishes for your Happy Holidays!

By Joanna Fuchs

Three Holidays

The end of the year brings a special gift:
Three holidays to give our spirits a lift.
Thanksgiving, (other holiday) and New Year's, too,
May they bring lots of pleasure and joy to you.

By Joanna Fuchs

Happy Holidays

It's the end of the year, and we're thinking of you;
We're searching for words, for the perfect phrase,
To let you know that you're special to us,
And to wish you and yours Happy Holidays!

By Joanna Fuchs

FATHER POEMS

General Father Poems

Life Lessons

You may have thought I didn't see,
Or that I hadn't heard,
Life lessons that you taught to me,
But I got every word.

Perhaps you thought I missed it all,
And that we'd grow apart,
But Dad, I picked up everything,
It's written on my heart.

Without you, Dad, I wouldn't be
The (woman)(man) I am today;
You built a strong foundation
No one can take away.

I've grown up with your values,
And I'm very glad I did;
So here's to you, dear father,
From your forever grateful kid.

By Joanna Fuchs

The Perfect Father

I love you because you're my father,
But you're really so much more;
You're a guide and a companion;
You and I have great rapport.

You pay attention to me;
You listen to what I say.
You pass on words of wisdom,
Helping me along the way.

Whenever I'm in trouble,
You always have a plan.

You are the perfect father,
And I'm your biggest fan!

By Karl and Joanna Fuchs

Glad You're My Dad

I'm so glad that you're my dad;
You're one in a million, Pop!
When it comes to first-class fathers,
You're the absolute cream of the crop.

You love me no matter what,
Whether I'm a goodie or baddie;
I really love you, Pa;
You're a fine and fantabulous daddy!

By Joanna Fuchs

Hero Dad

You are my hero, Dad
You're my secure foundation.
When I think of you, I'm filled with love
And fond appreciation.

You make me feel protected;
I'm sheltered by your care.
You're always my true friend, and Dad,
When I need you, you're always there.

You have a place of honor
Deep within my heart.
You've been my superhero, Dad,
Right from the very start.

By Joanna Fuchs

Perfect Dad Blend

I'm glad you're my father;
You're really the best;

As a dad, you're a fine one;
I'm so very blessed.

You're smart, and you're strong,
Just a perfect dad blend;
You're my father, my counselor
And a really good friend.

By Joanna Fuchs

My Father, My Guiding Light

Dad, you're like the sun to me,
a sure thing, always there,
beaming light and warmth on my life.
Whatever is good in me today,
I owe to your wisdom, your patience,
your strength, your love.
You taught me by example,
as a role model,
how to be my own person,
to believe in myself,
instructing me without controlling me.
Even when we disagreed,
you held us together,
so our bond was never broken.
I understand what you did for me,
and I am so grateful that I have you
as my solid foundation, my rock.
I respect you, I admire you, I love you,
my guiding light, my father.

By Joanna Fuchs

My Daddy Is The Greatest

My daddy is the greatest;
The best dad there ever was.
He always brings me lots of joy;
He's my very own Santa Claus.

My daddy can do anything;
He's smart as smart can be.
I love to walk and hold his hand
To show he belongs to me.

By Karl Fuchs

I'm Happy You're My Dad

I feel safe when you are with me;
You show me fun things to do;
You make my life much better;
The best father I know is you.

I'm happy you're my Dad
And so I want to say
I love you, Dad, and wish you
A Happy Father's Day!

By Joanna Fuchs

Star Dad

I love you, Dad, and want you to know,
I feel your love wherever I go.
Whenever I've problems, you're there to assist,
The ways you have helped me would make quite a list.

Your wisdom and knowledge have shown me the way,
And I'm thankful for you as I live day by day.
I don't tell you enough how important you are,
In my universe you're a bright shining star.

By Karl Fuchs

A Real Father

It's not so common anymore
to have a dad who's really there,
who is the provider for his family,
who comes home every night,
whose predictability
creates a sense of stability and security
in his household.
Your routine may not seem valuable to you,
but it's worth a lot to me.
I'm thankful that I can depend on you
to always be you--
a real father,
responsible, trustworthy,
and a great role model.

I've learned a lot of good things
from watching you.
Thanks, Dad.

By Joanna Fuchs

If Everyone Had a Father Like You

If everyone had a father
Who was more like you,
There'd be more laughing, joy and singing;
Fewer people would be blue.

There'd be much more understanding;
Crime and hate could not prevail;
We'd all be so contented,
We wouldn't need a jail.

If everyone had a father
Who was more like you,
The whole world would be blessed,
Just as I am blessed with you.

By Karl Fuchs

It's My Father

Do you know who I want to be like?
It's not Roosevelt, Reagan or Ike.
It's my father.

Who taught me to drive and skate?
Who taught me to care and not hate?
It's my father.

The man I'll respect till I die,
Who taught me always to try,
It's my father.

He was never too busy for me;
He's my ideal man, totally.
My father!

By Karl Fuchs

Terrific Father

You're a dad, and you're doing great;
At fatherly duties you star;
You deserve to celebrate
The terrific father you are.

You're doing a really wonderful job,
And so we'd like to convey
Our respect and admiration;
Happy Father's Day!

By Joanna Fuchs

First Father's Day Poem

So this is your first Father's Day,
Your first one as a dad;
Get ready for surprises now,
The wildest you've ever had.

Just when you think you've got it down,
There's a new and different stage;
This little person changes a lot
With each fascinating age.

Being a dad takes all you've got;
Your heart and mind you'll invest;
It's the hardest job you'll ever have,
And the one you'll love the best.

By Joanna Fuchs

Son to Father Poems

First-Class Father

Dad, I'm blessed to be your son
I knew it from the start.
You're a first-class father;
You're loving, kind, and smart.

You show me how to be a man

You help and guide me, along the way.
You're strong, and yet you're gentle, too.
I hope I'm just like you, someday!

By Joanna Fuchs

I'd Pick You

Dad, if all the fathers
Had lined up one by one,
And God told me I had to pick,
I'd still choose to be your son.

I'm proud to have a father
Who listens and understands,
Who teaches me and sets fair rules
Without unfair demands.

Dad you are my hero,
My role model in all you do.
So Dad, if I could pick again,
You know I'd still pick you!

By Joanna Fuchs

Daughter to Father Poems

Everything Dad

A little girl needs her daddy
To love her with manly charm,
To soothe her when she's hurt,
And keep her safe from harm.

A girl needs her dad
To show her a man who's good,
To help her make right choices,
As only a father could.

A woman needs her father
Just to be aware,
He'll always be there for her
To sustain her and to care.

You've been all these things, Dad.
I hope that you can see
How much I treasure you;
You mean everything to me.

By Joanna Fuchs

Always There For Your Daughter

Every day the whole year through,
I feel grateful you are my father.
Some fathers don't have time for their kids,
But for you I'm never a bother.

You always make the effort to listen and share;
You're there whenever you're needed.
Because I know how much you care,
My problems are defeated.

Dad, you are truly admired and adored,
And I hope you always know,
Your daughter's affection for you is strong,
And my love continues to grow.

By Joanna Fuchs

My Father Is My Hero

(Sung to the Tune of "When Irish Eyes Are Smiling")

My daddy was my hero
For my very youngest years;
Daddy kept me safe and happy,
And he chased away my fears.
I watched in awe and wonder
At each manly thing he did;
Oh, I looked up to my daddy,
When I was a little kid.

My dad was still my hero,
As the years passed, one by one.
He taught important lessons,
And he took some time for fun.

He was my firm foundation;
On my dad I did depend;
He was always there for me,
My dad, my guide, my friend.

My father is my hero,
Now that I am fully grown.
I love him and respect him,
The best man I've ever known.
I knew when I would marry
That my husband had to be
A great man, just like my father,
Dad, my hero you'll always be.

By Joanna Fuchs

Father's Day Poem From Wife

The Best Man I Ever Knew

When we married, I saw you as perfect,
The ideal husband and more;
I thought I knew all about you,
All the things to love and adore.

But when you became a father,
I saw new qualities to treasure.
You enrich all our lives in fresh ways;
As a dad, you bring so much pleasure.

Our children are forever blessed
To have a father like you,
And I love you more than ever,
You're the best man I ever knew.

By Joanna Fuchs

Stepfather Poem

Thanks for Being My Step dad

Although you are my step dad,
You're really so much more;
We get along so well;
We have great rapport.

You always listen to me;
I know you really care;
When I really need you
I know that you'll be there.

I'm learning really good things,
Just by watching you;
Thanks for being my step dad
And for being a good friend, too.

By Joanna Fuchs

Father-In-Law Poem

Special Father-In-Law

When I married I got a new father,
A special father in law;
That made me very happy,
And a little bit in awe.

You're an exceptional man who cares,
With an understanding heart.
You're also filled with wisdom;
No wonder my spouse is smart!

Thanks for being so cordial;
Thanks for welcoming me;
It feels really good to be part
Of your special family.

By Joanna Fuchs

Grandpa, You're the One

Grandpa you're the very best;
You're a lot of fun.
When I need someone to care,
Grandpa you're the one.

You're always in a real good mood.
I'm happy when you're with me;
I love you, and I always will,
You're the best grandpa that could be!

By Joanna Fuchs

My Special Joy

A grandfather is a special blessing
enriching the life of a grandchild
with unique and incomparable joys.
Grandpa, you are my special joy.
I get a warm, safe, contented feeling
when I think of you.
With you, I feel no pressure to be
what someone else wants me to be;
you love me enough to let me be me.
You're never in a hurry;
you always take time to listen and to help.
You are always there for me when I need you;
You're never too busy for talks, for walks.
I can count on your wisdom,
your life experience,
your understanding heart
to help me comprehend and get through
challenges you've already faced.
You are part parent, part teacher,
part best friend.
Your strength and your easy, calm confidence
is your legacy to me,
and I love you dearly.

By Joanna Fuchs

Poem for Deceased Father

We Can't Believe You're Gone

Dad, our sadness knows no end;
We can't believe you're gone;
We're grieving for you every day;
It's hard to carry on.

You were always there to support and care,
When we needed a true friend,
How we'll ever do without our dad,
We cannot comprehend.

You were our teacher and our guide,
Our dad, so good and strong;
Your example will sustain us now,
And last our whole lives long.

We're trying to communicate;
We hope that you can hear;
Expressing what we feel for you,
Helps us feel you're near.

Our memories of the times we had
Help the pain to go away.
But Dad, our lives won't be the same;
We'll miss you every day.

A part of us went with you;
You left a gap too big to fill;
You're our father and our hero;
We love you and we always will.

By Joanna Fuchs

Christian Father's Day Poem

My Father Is A Christian

My father is a Christian;
He leads our household well;
With instruction from the Bible,
Right behavior he'll compel.

Yet he steers us with compassion;
His gentle love is true;
He conforms to our Lord Jesus,
So we know just what to do.

He teaches us with purpose,
Guides us in all Godly ways,
So we will take the right path,
And serve our Lord with praise.

I'm glad you're a Christian, Dad;
You help me see things clearly.
I'll always look up to you,
And love you very dearly.

By Joanna Fuchs

Father's Day Prayer

Bless Our Fathers

Lord, please bless our fathers,
these men who mean so much to us,
who are greatly responsible
for who we are and who we are becoming.
Bless them for having the courage
to do what's necessary to keep us out of trouble,
for making us do the right thing,
for helping us build our character,
even when it makes us angry;
and bless them for pushing us to do our best,
even when they just want to love us.
Bless our fathers for being our protectors,
for leading us through stormy times to safety,
for making us believe that everything will be all right
and for making it so.
Bless our fathers for quietly making a living
to provide for those they love most,
for giving us food, clothing, shelter
and the other material things that really matter,
for unselfishly investing time and money in us
that they could have spent on themselves.

Bless our fathers, Lord,
for saving some energy for fun,
for leading us on adventures
to explore the outer reaches of ourselves,
for making us laugh,
for being our playmates and our friends.
Bless them for being our secure foundation, our rock,
for holding on tight to us...until it's time to let us go.
Lord, bless these men we look up to,
our role models, our heroes,
our fathers.
In Jesus' name we pray, Amen.

By Joanna Fuchs

FRIENDSHIP POEMS

General Friendship Poems

Thank You, Friend

Thank you, friend, for all the things
That mean so much to me--
For concern and understanding
You give abundantly.

Thanks for listening with your heart,
For cheering me when I'm blue,
For bringing out the best in me,
And just for being you.

Thanks for in-depth conversation
That stimulates my brain,
For silly times we laugh out loud,
For things I can't explain.

For looking past my flaws and faults,
For all the time you spend,
For all the kind things that you do,
Thank you, thank you, friend.

By Joanna Fuchs

My Everything Friend

You magnify my happiness
When I am feeling glad;
You help to heal my injured heart
Whenever I am sad.

You're such a pleasure in my life;
I hope that you can see
How meaningful your friendship is;
You're a total joy to me.

By Joanna Fuchs

Truly A Friend

Someone to lean on when problems appear,
Someone on whom you'd depend,
Someone who'll lift you when you're down in the dumps,
That someone is truly a friend.

That's how I feel about you my dear friend;
You're so special just as you are.
Just to know that you're there provides comfort to spare;
A friendship like yours sets the bar.

By Karl and Joanna Fuchs

Because you are my friend

Because you are my friend,
my life is enriched in a myriad of ways.
Like a cool breeze on a sweltering day,
like a ray of sunshine parting glowering clouds,
you lift me up.
In good times, we soar,
like weightless balloons over neon rainbows.
In bad times, you are soothing balm
for my pummeled soul.
I learn so much from you;
you help me see old things in new ways.
I wonder if you are aware
of the bright seeds you are sowing in me.
I'm a better person for knowing you,
so that everyone I interact with
is touched by your good effect on me.
You relax me, refresh me, renew me.
Your bounteous heart envelops me
in joy and love and peace.
May your life be filled
with dazzling blessings,
just as I am blessed
by being your friend.

By Joanna Fuchs

My Treasured Friend

Treasured friend, I'm glad I found you;
Our friendship is a gift we share.
I can be myself around you,
Safe in your love and care.

I miss you when you're out of sight;
Our friendship bond was meant to be.
I think of you with great delight;
You're almost part of me.

Through fun and fears, play and tears,
We help each other heal and grow.
I prize our time--the days, the years,
More than you can know.

Just harmony for me and you,
The two of us--a perfect blend.
I'll cherish you my whole life through,
My dear and treasured friend.

By Joanna Fuchs

A Friend I Can Count On

When troubles come a callin'
As those gremlins often do,
And my spirit keeps on fallin'
Till I feel low down and blue,

When I look around for comfort,
Someone quickly jumps to mind,
One who always will support me,
And whose words are always kind,

Who will make my mood feel lighter,
Who'll help beat my troubles back,
He makes the sun shine brighter,
And gets my spirit back on track,

Who helps the road seem straighter,
And helps me get around each bend,
Who makes each day seem greater,
And that someone is you, my friend.

By Karl Fuchs

Friendship Joy

You are a shelter
From life's frequent storm;
Like a comfortable blanket;
You keep me snug, safe and warm.

You're a light in the window
When everything's dark;
You're a trip to the circus,
A romp in the park.

Like a bright, sunny summer,
You are joy without end;
And I'm so very privileged
To call you my friend.

By Joanna Fuchs

We Are Friends

Whether the day is good or bad,
Whether I'm feeling happy or sad,
If I have a need, you'll comprehend;
You'll be there to share and be a friend.

Other people may fill my day,
But never in such an important way;
We support each other 'round all of life's bends,
It feels so good that we are friends.

By Karl Fuchs

Pure Delight

It's such a pleasure and a joy
To have a friend like you.
You always care, you're always there,
You say the right things, too!

You make me smile when I am low
You're just a pure delight.
We talk a lot about everything;
You make my life so bright!

I hope that I am giving you
Some joy and happiness,
Because you mean so much to me,
More than I can express!

By Joanna Fuchs

My Giving Friend

We share so much of our lives
Our joy and also our pain.
Without you as my friend,
I just might go insane!

You know what I'm talking about;
You've been through big things, too.
Yet you cheer me when I'm happy,
You comfort me when I'm blue.

Your giving does not go unnoticed;
I'd be lost without you, friend.
What we have together
No one else can comprehend.

By Joanna Fuchs

The Power of Friends

Everyone knows of the power of friends,
The terrific result, when everything blends.
When people have friends, they don't stand alone;
Friends always help, when you face the unknown.

Friends give you courage to face problems untold,
So the love of a friend can help make you bold.
They can help you to live a much richer life,
So your every day living will be less filled with strife.

By Karl and Joanna Fuchs

Dream Friend

I always dreamed someone swell would turn up,
Who'd consider my feelings routinely,
Who would share lots of stuff without being gruff,
And if they disagreed would not do it meanly.

Then you came along and my wishes came true;
You're a friend who I trust and I treasure.
You always give help and I know that you care;
You're my friend and it gives me great pleasure.

By Karl and Joanna Fuchs

GET WELL POEMS

Magic Wand

I wish I had a magic wand
To make it go away;
I'd be with you, right by your side,
And wave it every day.

I'd think good thoughts; I'd send you love;
I'd transmit healing vibes;
My wand and I would surely beat
Whatever the doc prescribes.

There is no magic scepter, so
I cannot cast a spell.
Just know you're often in my thoughts,
And I hope you'll soon be well!

By Joanna Fuchs

Hang In There

Hello, my friend; you're on my mind,
Because you're somehow ailing,
But your response to any challenge
Has always been unfailing.

So I'm confident you'll win again;
Hang in there, and you'll see;
You'll be back on top in no time,
Tackling life courageously.

By Joanna Fuchs

Think Good Thoughts

Being sick has a mental part,
So use your head to cure you.

Thinking good thoughts is the way to start,
And smiling works, I assure you.

Keep up your spirits to cheer yourself;
Don't let the gloomies win.
A happy soul will get well fast,
And right now is the time to begin.

By Karl Fuchs

Get Mended!

Illness means something's not working quite right,
So do what it takes to get mended.
When you are sick, it gives me quite a fright,
So please, let your illness be ended!

By Karl and Joanna Fuchs

When You're Not Here

When you are ill,
our sun goes under a cloud.
Your presence in our lives is such a bright joy
that everything seems in shadow
when you're not here.
When you aren't feeling well,
we feel the lack of your glowing energy
and contagious vitality.
When you are sick, we feel incomplete,
like a jigsaw puzzle with a missing piece;
Please rest, take good care of yourself,
and feel better.
We miss you and want you back.

By Joanna Fuchs

Bad Bug

Has a bad bug gotten hold of you,
Making you feel queasy?

You're energy's low, you're indisposed,
Being sick's not easy!

Just take this opportunity
To recuperate and rest,
And then when you return to us
You'll be your very best!

By Joanna Fuchs

Get Well

Get well, get well, whatever you have;
We miss your great charm and fine wit.
There's plenty of time to be ill later on,
So let's see you back, well and fit!

By Karl and Joanna Fuchs

When You're Gone

We miss you when you're gone.
We miss the sparkling light you shine
into the shadowy corners of our days.
You're not up to being your amazing self,
and although we know this is temporary,
we selfishly want you back, right now.
We need your bright spirit, your love of life
to lift us up, as you always do, effortlessly,
just by being you.
Please take care of yourself and recover soon.
We miss you when you're gone.

By Joanna Fuchs

I Care

I'm sending this to let you know
I think of you each day,
And pray for your recovery,
Hoping soon you'll be okay.

You're going through a lot right now;
You're treatments can be trying;
Remember while you do them
It's your problem you're defying.

Hold on to your positive attitude,
And when things get hard to bear,
Know that I am here for you;
Remember that I care.

And when you're well and flourishing,
Look back and realize,
You learned what you were made of;
That's a reward that satisfies!

By Joanna Fuchs

You Are Deeply Missed

Get well real fast, my friend,
That's what I wish for you,
For while you're sick you're deeply missed,
So I am sad and blue.

So have some pity on me,
Don't leave me in the dump.
Return to health real soon, my friend,
Or I will be a grump!

By Karl Fuchs

Take It Easy

I am so sorry
to hear that you are ill.
Know that I am thinking of you often
and praying for your quick recovery.
Take it easy, rest,
and be kind to yourself,
and if there's anything you need,
call me first.
I miss you, care about you
and look forward to seeing you restored
to perfect health.

By Joanna Fuchs

Bring Back Your Special Spark

I hear you're feeling not so well;
It's no fun being sickly.
Please know I care about you,
And hope you get well quickly.

When you're gone, you're sorely missed;
A bit of my world turns dark;
So take good care, recuperate,
And bring back your special spark!

By Joanna Fuchs

Please Feel Better

Feel better and get back to yourself before long;
When you're ill, I hurt 'cause I care.
Whenever you're sick, a part of me mourns;
I keep thinking that life isn't fair.

I worry about you and wish you the best,
Please get well and become safe and sound.
That will give me new hope, and I won't need to mope,
When I see that you're up and around.

By Karl and Joanna Fuchs

Get Well Soon

I hope you're feeling better;
I miss you every day.
I'm always thinking of you,
So this is what I say:
Get Well Soon!

By Karl Fuchs

Get Back To Work!

Get well quick, you lazy bum,
There's lots of work to do.
If you stay sick, it's more work for me,
And I'd rather it was for you.

By Karl Fuchs

Come Back

Why you chose this particular time to get sick,
Seems to us an insensitive choice.
So don't be so selfish; don't be a sloth;
Come back so we all can rejoice!

By Karl Fuchs

All In Your Head

Let's go, get up, stop faking it;
Get your sorry behind off that bed.
Try positive thinking to get back to work.
Your illness is all in your head!

By Karl and Joanna Fuchs

GRADUATION POEMS

Your Adventure

Now that you've graduated,
Your adventure has begun.
Your schooling has prepared you
For the race life has you run.

We praise you for your efforts,
And send good wishes, too,
For a future filled with happiness,
And your fondest dreams come true.

By Joanna Fuchs

Always Be A Student

Keep on learning, (graduate's name),
Though your graduation's done;
Your whole life's an education
That has only just begun.

Your diploma is the first big step,
For knowledge is the special key
To winning what you want in life
And being who you want to be.

If you'll always be a student,
You'll find the secrets to success,
And cruise right down the road
To peace and happiness.

By Joanna Fuchs

If You Believe

Your diploma means a future without boundaries,
A world that's full of energy and fun.
So as you reach for all life has to offer,
Remember that you're second to no one.

Pursue your goals, yet keep your loved ones close,
As you utilize your talent and ambition.
Let your friends and family give you their support,
And you'll master every challenging transition.

And always, (graduate's name), know you can achieve
The things you really want, if you believe.

By Joanna Fuchs

Bright Future

Now that you've graduated
Nothing can stop you now.
You've worked hard to get your diploma;
It's time to take a bow.

Congratulations graduate!
Your future looks strong and bright.
May you achieve the things you hope for
And have a life of sheer delight.

By Joanna Fuchs

On Wings of Knowledge

There you are in your cap and tassel
Ready to make the world your castle.
It seems just yesterday you were a kid,
Watching everything we did.

Now we're watching you graduate--
The grown young woman we helped create!
On wings of knowledge you will fly;
Following your vision and rising high.

We couldn't be prouder, (graduate's name), of you;
We wish you success in all you do.
Remember one thing we want you to know:
Our love is with you wherever you go.

By Joanna Fuchs

A New Beginning

As you make a new beginning in your life, graduate,
Be aware of important things you didn't learn in school:

As you pursue your dreams,
Remember to take time to help and serve others,
even if doing so slows you down a little.
As you explore and develop your unique talents,
remain humble,
realizing that your special abilities are gifts from God.
As life hands you challenges, welcome them
as ways to become smarter and stronger.
As you acquire material things,
know that your most important possessions
are honesty, integrity,
and the desire to make a difference.
Congratulations, graduate.
May your new path take you where you want to go
and also bring you pleasant surprises!

By Joanna Fuchs

You Stand Out

If every single graduate
Were as special as you are,
The world would be a better place
And everyone a star.

In the real world, though,
You sure stand out
For your extraordinary traits,
Those uncommon things about you
Everyone appreciates.

So congratulations, graduate!
We wish you all the best.
We know as you meet life's challenges,
You'll ace each and every test!

By Joanna Fuchs

The Special Door

It took a lot of work,
Time, and persistence, too,
To achieve the important goal
That you set out to do.

Your effort now pays off,
The world now offers more.
To you, new graduate,
It opens a special door.

Congratulations (Name of graduate),
You did it all; you made it through.
You took your first step toward success,
And we're so proud of you!

By Joanna Fuchs

Graduation Friendship

We're graduating, and we know
Our lives will be different and new;
We're going out into the world,
Our goals and dreams to pursue.

But one thing will never, ever change,
As we go our separate ways;
The friends we've made in school will be
Our friends for all our days.

The special ties and attachments we've made,
These bonds will never be broken;
We'll continue to feel that special bond,
Though words may not be spoken.

So it's not "goodbye," but rather "farewell;"
I'll see you again, my friend.
Your friendship means a lot to me,
And it will never end.

By Joanna Fuchs

College Graduation Poem

Awesome Achievement

Your college graduation
Fills us with love and pride.
We always knew that you could do
Whatever you really tried.

It's a long and challenging journey
To get a college degree,
But you wouldn't quit it, you just went and did it,
And we're beaming affectionately.

Your achievement is awesome, (graduate's name);
You've worked hard and you've passed the test.
We love you so, and we want you to know,
We think you're the very best!

By Joanna Fuchs

Graduation Gift Thank You

Graduation Thank You

Thank you for the gift you gave
For my (8th grade/high school/college) graduation;
Thank you for acknowledging
This special celebration.

I'm grateful for your thoughtfulness;
I appreciate your present;
Thanks for making this eventful time
More joyful and more pleasant!

By Joanna Fuchs

Graduation Invitation

Significant Occasion

(Name) is graduating from (high school, college)
Please tell us you'll be there;
This significant occasion
Is an event we'd like to share.

Please come to this graduation;
To see you is always a pleasure.
Your presence in the audience
Would be something we would treasure!

By Joanna Fuchs

Preschool and Kindergarten Graduation Poems

The Next School

You did great work we're proud to say,
You did it, and you're on your way.
The next school will be fun for you,
And it's something we know that you can do!

By Karl Fuchs

Work Is Play

Everyone is proud of what you've done,
You've learned a lot and had some fun.
Now there's more school up ahead,
Just make your work seem like play instead.

And if you play the game that way,
How far you'll go, no one can say.

By Karl Fuchs

You've Done Your Job

Now it's time to graduate
You did well, and that is great
You've done your job, and we're so proud,
We want to dance and shout out loud!

By Karl Fuchs

Christian Graduation Poem

The Lord Will Lead You

Now that you're celebrating
Your graduation day,
Your whole life is ahead of you,
And the Lord will lead the way.

Just trust in Him to guide you
In His divine and perfect will.
If you'll pray and read His Holy Word,
His plan you will fulfill.

Whatever happens in your life,
On the Lord you can depend.
There's nothing you can't handle
With Jesus as your best friend.

By Joanna Fuchs

Graduation Songs

Graduation Song

(To the Tune of "Morning Has Broken")

We're graduating
Into our future,
Anticipating
Only the best.
Spreading our wings now
We'll do great things now,

Meet every challenge
Pass every test.

We'll overcome what-
ever life hands us,
Use what we learned here
For our success.
We'll bloom wherever
Our journey lands us,
Reaching our goal of
Sweet happiness.

Friendships we made here
Will be unbroken;
Though words aren't spoken,
Feelings are strong.
Memories we treasure
Tie us together,
Recalling pleasure
All our lives long.

We're thankful for our
Good education;
Our school and teachers
Are second to none.
We'd like to give them
Appreciation;
We learned a lot, and
We thank everyone.

By Joanna Fuchs

We Are Graduating Now

(Sung to the Tune of "Come Now Fount of Every Blessing")

We are graduating now, and
Things are coming to an end.
We appreciate our teachers,
And we'll never lose a friend.
We will remember what we learned here;
We will remember everything.
And when we are gone from this place,
To our memories we'll cling.

Education is the best thing
That we ever will possess.
We will use what our school taught us
To achieve our own success.
We are connected to our friends and school;
We are connected to it all.
When we think about our school days,
Only good things we'll recall.

So goodbye now to our school days,
To the children we once were.
All the things we thought and did here
Will become a pleasant blur.
We say hello now to our future;
We say hello to what will be.
We all have what we all need; our
Education sets us free.

By Joanna Fuchs

Graduation Song for Young Children

(To the Tune of "Farmer in the Dell")

We're graduating now;
We're graduating now;
We're going to a (insert grade) class;
We're graduating now.

We'll learn some new things there;
We'll learn some new things there;
We're going to have a lot of fun;
We'll learn some new things there.

We'll meet and make good friends;
We'll meet and make good friends;
We'll like them, and they'll like us, too;
We'll meet and make good friends;

Our teacher will be nice;
Our teacher will be nice.
She'll teach us what we need to know;
Our teacher will be nice.

We're graduating now;
We're graduating now;
We're going to a (insert grade) class;
We're graduating now.

By Joanna Fuchs

Graduation Prayer

Bless These Graduates

Dear Lord,
Please bless these graduates
as they go out into the world
to make it a better place,
while they pursue their dreams.
Gently guide them, lead them,
show them Your way to success and happiness
through service to others,
as they maximize their own potential.
Fill them with joy when they reach their goals.
Strengthen them, as they deal with life's obstacles,
and show them that every challenge
is a path to character development.
Give them the intelligence
to make a plan for their futures.
Give them the patience and persistence
to pursue their ambitions.
Most of all, give them caring hearts
to look for ways to help the people they meet
on their life's journey.
Encourage them and lift them up now,
as they spread their wings
into a clear sky of limitless opportunity.
Let each and every graduate here
be wrapped in the warmth of Your infinite love,
and let Your wisdom show them the way
to make the most of their lives.
In Jesus' name we pray, Amen.

By Joanna Fuchs

LOVE POEMS

If Not For You

If not for you, I wouldn't know
What true love really meant.
I'd never feel this inner peace;
I couldn't be content.

If not for you, I'd never have
The pleasures of romance.
I'd miss the bliss, the craziness,
Of love's sweet, silly dance.

I have to feel your tender touch;
I have to hear your voice;
No other one could take your place;
You're it; I have no choice.

If not for you, I'd be adrift;
I don't know what I'd do;
I'd be searching for my other half,
Incomplete, if not for you.

By Joanna Fuchs

Creatures of the Fire

We swan-dive into the volcano, burning;
We're creatures of the fire,
Mingled male and female, yearning
For the heat, the sweet explosion of desire.

I splash into the pleasure, all consuming;
I'm joyfully insane,
My passion for you deep, and fully blooming;
Long after, sweet warm flickers still remain.

You make my body sizzle with your kisses,
And yet there's so much more;

My heart is kindled, too; It knows what bliss is,
This closeness that I've never felt before.

My body and my heart belong to you;
I'm peaceful and complete.
I see more adventures coming for we two,
We creatures of the tender fire and heat.

By Joanna Fuchs

Reasons Why

Our love is the long lasting kind;
We've been together quite awhile.
I love you for so many things,
Your voice, your touch, your kiss, your smile.

You accept me as I am;
I can relax and just be me.
Even when my quirks come out,
You think they're cute; you let me be.

With you, there's nothing to resist;
You're irresistible to me.
I'm drawn to you in total trust;
I give myself to you willingly.

Your sweet devotion never fails;
You view me with a patient heart.
You love me, dear, no matter what.
You've been that way right from the start.

Those are just a few reasons why
I'll always love you like I do.
We'll have a lifetime full of love,
And it will happen because of you.

By Joanna Fuchs

No One Loves Me Like You Do

No one loves me like you do;
I've never felt like this;
You please me in so many ways,
With a word, a caress, a kiss.

No one understands me like you do;
You see me deep inside,
You choose to overlook my flaws,
The ones I try to hide.

No one satisfies me like you do,
When our bodies intertwine;
You give so much with your tender touch,
You're amazing, and you're mine!

No one loves me like you do;
You fill my every need,
And that is why, my darling,
I'll follow wherever you lead.

By Joanna Fuchs

Because of You

I was self sufficient,
gratified by my independence,
alone, but not lonely...I thought.
But I was restless,
searching blindly for something
to fill an empty place
I didn't even know I had,
dimly aware
that I was somehow unfinished.
Then you came, and filled everything,
every space, every need,
even secret dreams
I had concealed from myself.
I was self sufficient, and restless;
Now I am profoundly peaceful
and complete,
because of you.

By Joanna Fuchs

Safe Within Our Love

How did this miracle happen
That we're so very blessed,
So close…and more contented,
Than I ever would have guessed.

I never thought that I
Could spend each precious minute
With just one special person
And find happiness within it.

I've learned so much from you
About loving, sharing, giving;
I know if I hadn't met you,
I wouldn't be really living.

We're facing life together;
We're handling joy and sorrow;
I'm glad you're on my side,
Whatever comes tomorrow.

You're my perfect partner,
Sweet lover, trusted friend.
We're safe within our love,
A love that will never end.

By Joanna Fuchs

Never Like This

I've held others before,
But it was never like this,
Where my body inhales you
And quivers with bliss,

Where my senses are reeling
From the strength of desire,
And if I can't have you soon,
I'll be consumed by the fire.

By Karl Fuchs

A Love Song

Let me sing you a love song
About what I feel in my heart;
Butterflies can't find nectar
Whenever we're apart.

You're a flower in bloom.
In the dark, in the gloom,
It's you who brightens my day.
How many ways do I need you?
Every day, every way, come what may.

By Karl Fuchs

Always

I always yearn to come to you,
be with you,
connect with you,
unite with you,
merge with you.
I always love to nurture you,
nourish you,
meet your needs,
feed your hungers.
I will always cherish you,
treasure you,
adore you.
I always want to be yours,
Always.

By Joanna Fuchs

One In A Million

You're one in a million, my most special one;
Your radiant smile is as bright as the sun;
You're smart and caring and have many great charms,
And my heart really sings when you're in my arms.

I'm happy you chose me from all of the rest,
And I'm proud 'cause I know that I got the best.
You're so cute and so sweet, and you glow like a pearl;
I just love you so much, my most wonderful girl!

By Karl Fuchs

You Just Keep On Loving Me

No matter what I look like,
Whether pretty or plain you see,
When I'm all dressed up or in PJs,
You just keep on loving me.

Sometimes I'm happy and cheerful;
Other times grumpy and sad;
Your absolute love never wavers,
Whether I'm grouchy or glad.

Sometimes I try to change you;
And sometimes I criticize;
But I feel something melting within me,
When I see all the love in your eyes.

Your tolerance is endless,
However I choose to be;
Having my love makes you happy,
So you just keep on loving me.

And that is why, my darling,
Whatever else I do,
One thing is sure; no matter what,
I'll just keep on loving you.

By Joanna Fuchs

Beautiful

My thoughts of you are like raindrops on flowers...
Beautiful.
My thoughts of you are like a rainbow at a splashing waterfall...
Beautiful.
My thoughts of you are like a full moon
shining through a cloudy night sky...
Beautiful.
No matter what wonders my eyes have seen,
Nothing compares to the beauty I see
when I look at you.
My love for you is beautiful.

By Karl Fuchs

I Think Of You

When I think of you, you fill my mind;
There's no more thinking room I find.
I've never had such thoughts before;
I'm lost in you, whom I adore.

I think no more of mundane things,
Like common pleasures that living brings.
I just think of you, and I'm filled with dreams;
To keep your love fills all my schemes.

By Karl Fuchs

Lucky

We all are explorers on the great sea of life;
We search and we hunt for our pleasure.
Some adventures are fruitful, and some disappoint,
But few find a gem they can treasure.

I'm so blessed I found you as my priceless prize;
You're a treasure in every way.
I searched with the rest and discovered the best;
Finding you was my luckiest day.

By Karl and Joanna Fuchs

Beware

When love strikes us hard and makes mush of our brain,
When love sneaks in and makes us insane,
All sense can depart and leave the brain blank,
When love like that strikes it can drain our whole tank.

So beware of the power you exert over me,
For I'm under your spell; that's clear as can be.
Whenever you're near, my brain slips out of joint;
I could fight my love, but what is the point?

You're my strength and my weakness, for I love you so dearly,
And I hope our love shines through the years just as clearly.

By Karl Fuchs

All The Things I Love About You

I love you for the sweet affection in your eyes
whenever you look at me,
and the special smile you save only for me.
I love that you always seek
to have your body close to mine,
reaching out to touch, to hold my hand,
to wrap your arms around me.
I love how you show me you care
by looking for ways
to make my life easier and more comfortable.
I love that when I ask you to do things,
you try to do them
instead of thinking me demanding.
I love that your favorite place is near me,
that you'd rather be with me than anywhere else.
I love you for more reasons
than this page has space to write,
so I'll try to tell you and show you in person
all the things I love about you.

By Joanna Fuchs

The Prisoner

What is it about you that makes me feel weak,
And gives me the goose bumps whenever you speak?
Why does the sight of you fill me with pleasure,
Like a spotlight that shines on a glorious treasure?

Are you so different from others I've known?
What qualities do you have that are yours alone?
What can it be that fills up my heart?
And makes me feel lost whenever we part?

There's no easy answer for this marvelous bliss,
For the wonder I feel whenever we kiss,
For the fire that rages at the touch of your skin,
For the way my heart pounds for you way deep within.

It must be the power of love that I feel,
That ties me in bonds that seem strong as steel.
I could fight to get loose, but I'd rather give in;
To stay trapped by your charms is how I will win.

By Karl and Joanna Fuchs

I'm Writing It Down

Sometimes a man's mind and tongue
seem disconnected.
My mind realizes your wonderfulness,
but my tongue might fail to tell you.
Maybe, since my eyes and brain
see how very obvious
your lovely, endearing qualities are,
my tongue thinks
I don't need to let you know.
In case there is any doubt
about what I am thinking and feeling,
I am writing it down for you:
I always think
you are the prettiest, smartest,
most wonderful, kindest,
most loveable girl
in all the world.
I want to hug, kiss, love
and adore you forever.
Please try to have patience
with the negligence of my tongue.
I am working to keep it in the loop better.

By Karl and Joanna Fuchs

You Let Me Be Me

While others tell me I have faults and flaws,
And pick me all apart and criticize,
You love me, sweetheart, just the way I am;
I only see affection in your eyes.

My pesky quirks you only find endearing;
Your perfect mate is what you choose to see;
I love you for a multitude of reasons;
And most of all 'cause you let me be me.

I never have to change to meet your standards;
Acceptance is the greatest gift you give;
I appreciate you for your sweet devotion,
And I'll love you for as long as we shall live.

By Joanna Fuchs

A Dream Fulfilled

How could anyone ever know,
The sweet dreams that I dreamed as a youth,
Could blossom and focus and grow,
Until now they'd turn up as a truth.

A truth filled with blessing and wonder,
A truth filled with love and with caring,
A truth with a voice loud as thunder,
A truth with a message worth sharing.

For you, my love, filled all my dreams,
Of a life I thought never could be.
Now with you at my side, I'm contented;
For my dreaming came true, don't you see?

I never gave up on my dreaming,
I persisted because I just knew,
A wait for real love is worth waiting,
Now you're here, and my dreams have come true.

By Karl Fuchs

My Girl with the Reddish Hair

Pirates bold in days of old
Searched the world for treasure rare,
But none they found as bright and sound,
As my girl with the reddish hair.

Precious gold and sparkling jewels
Were fortunes to make men care,
But none were worth a penny
Next to my girl with the reddish hair.

These pirates fought and died for wealth;
Their lives I wouldn't share,
For I have the only wealth I need:
My girl with the reddish hair.

By Joanna Fuchs

The Wizard

There's a story told of a wizard
Who, for money, would cast a spell,
And I'm sure that you met this wizard,
And you, his wares he did sell.

What else can explain how your smile
Can make my heartbeat roar,
Or how your look slows my breathing,
While causing my spirits to soar.

I'm sure that you and this wizard
Conspired to control my brain,
For I'm always thinking about you--
Feeling happy and slightly insane.

Now I hope I meet that same wizard,
For I'd give him all of my gold,
To make you want to stay with me,
And share happiness as we grow old.

By Karl Fuchs

The Dream Road

I've had a dream, since I was young
Of just how life should be,
But through the years, try as I might,
That dream eluded me.

I dreamed of a life that was filled with bliss;
I dreamed of love and sharing.
I dreamed, imagined and creatively planned
An adventure for two who were caring.

The road to today was paved with the dreams
That slowly got ground to dust.
And I've trudged that road and carried my load
And tried very hard to adjust.

Each step made me stronger; each test made me wiser,
So on my long walk, I grew,
Till the time was right, one magical night,
For the road to make room for two.

Now my brain shouts your name, and your loving reply
Makes a place for you in my heart.
(Name), it cries--so tender, so wise--
Let's make the adventure start!

Together we're blessed with a perfect match,
Something that's bright and new.
It's not too late, so let's create
A life that makes dreams come true.

By Karl Fuchs

Until I Met You

Before I met you, I thought I was happy,
and I was,
but I had never known the rich contentment,
deep satisfaction, and total fulfillment
you brought to me, when you came into my life.
Before I met you, I felt a lot of things,
good things,
but I had never experienced
the indescribably intense feelings I have for you.
Before I met you, I thought I knew myself,
and I did,
but you looked deep inside me
and found fresh new things for us to share.
Before I met you, I thought I knew about love,
but I didn't,
until I met you.

By Joanna Fuchs

Daydreams

My thoughts of you come frequently;
They're always filled with you and me.
No matter what I see or when,
It brings you back to mind again.

I'd be sitting, reading a book,
Or be out walking by a brook;

No matter what the path I took,
I'd see dream images of how you look.

Each day is filled with dreams of you;
I hope that all these dreams come true.

By Karl Fuchs

Teen Love Poems

Invisible

I see you at school
And you glance my way,
Passing in the halls
In your ordinary day.

But anytime
Your eyes meet mine
Is a day so rare,
A day so fine.

Just another face,
I'm nothing to you;
You look but don't see;
You haven't a clue...

That my heart is racing;
I'm trembling inside;
So much love for you
I'm trying to hide.

You smile at others;
You pass me by;
I'm invisible,
And I want to cry.

By Joanna Fuchs

Just Friends?

You say that you like me,
But that we're just friends;

Can I feel the same?
Well I think it depends:

Can I quit breathing fast
Each time you appear?
Will my heart stop its pounding
Whenever you're near?

I'd like to feel nothing,
And get rid of the thrill.
I wish I'd stop loving you,
But I don't think I will.

By Joanna Fuchs

Relationship Poems

Love Can Stay Strong

When love first comes and all seems right;
It's beyond our reason that we two can fight.
Yet fights will come, and anger might thrive,
So let's try to be sure that our love will survive.

Let's make our plans with similar goals,
So our wants and desires won't hit hidden shoals
That set us crashing when things get hard,
So our love can stay strong even when it gets jarred.

For if love can stay strong when it's tested by fire,
Then we'd share a future that most would admire,
A future where partners would strive side by side,
A future where love would always abide.

By Karl and Joanna Fuchs

The Lover's Quarrel

For many years we've lived and loved,
Our lives a rich delight.
Then one day's events caused us to clash,
And the friction led to a fight.

You think that words can't do a lot,
But words are not inert.
Words have the power to sooth and calm,
But can also cut and hurt.

If thoughts are kept within your head,
They can be dealt with by you alone.
But once the words are past your lips,
They're like a monument carved in stone.

So always take the time to think,
Of the hurt that can take place,
Whenever a thought is hastily said,
To cause someone loss of face.

It's hard work to tear the monument down,
To make the hurtful words lose their power.
It's so much better not to speak the thought,
And just complain to yourself for an hour.

By Karl Fuchs

Sad Love Poems

If I'd Never Met You

If I'd never met you,
I wouldn't feel the pain
Of losing your sweet love;
I wouldn't feel insane.

But if I'd never met you,
I wouldn't know the pleasure
Of ecstasy's warm gifts
And memories to treasure.

Now moving on with life,
I force a wistful grin,
Questioning what went wrong
And wondering what might have been.

By Joanna Fuchs

Farewell My Love

Is it really true our love is over now?
Can it be time for us to say goodbye?
Too soon, it's much too soon, my love, for me;
You smile with ease, but I can only sigh.

We've shared our lives and given so much love;
I can't believe we're really going to part;
You're moving toward a new life without me;
I'm left with scars upon my broken heart.

Go on now, if you must; I'll get along;
How much it hurts, I don't want you to know.
I'll set you free without inducing guilt,
But as you leave, the silent tears will flow.

I can't be mad; I love you way too much;
I'll hide my sadness now, so you can't tell.
Sweet happiness is what I wish for you;
Farewell my love, I hope that you fare well.

By Joanna Fuchs

Is This What Love Is?

Is this all we have together?
Is this what love really is,
Yelling through a quarrel
And making up with a kiss?

Why can't we get along?
Why do we have to fight?
We starve true love by day
And feed lust all through the night.

I wish we'd settle down;
I wonder where peace went.
Why do we pick at each other;
Why can't we be content?

If this is what love is,
If tenderness has flown,
I'm thinking more and more,
It's better to be alone.

By Joanna Fuchs

You Were My Everything

You were my everything;
Now you're gone.
I don't have the strength
To carry on.

Skies always seemed sunny
When you were here;
Now there's nothing but gloom
In my atmosphere.

I loved you so much;
You were all I had;
Now my whole world
Is depressing and sad.

I'd like to start feeling
Other than blue,
But you were my everything,
What can I do?

By Joanna Fuchs

Is It Enough?

When we converse, it's just surface stuff;
We say some words, but is it enough?
We get along; we rarely fight,
But where is the spark, the joy, the delight?
We're settled into the same routine;
Sometimes I'd like to flee this scene.
Everything's easy; we don't have it rough,
But sometimes I wonder: Is it enough?

By Joanna Fuchs

Now That You're Gone

Now that you're gone, I realize
How much you meant to me.
My loss is wide as a starless night sky,
And deep as a stormy sea.

I miss the comfort of your sweet love,
Your absolute devotion;
Now I'm a fountain of endless tears,
A pool of sad emotion.

They tell me I should move on with life,
That time will heal my pain;
I smile and nod and agree with them,
While I slowly go insane.

By Joanna Fuchs

If Only

If only I had done the things
That keep true love alive,
I wouldn't have to acknowledge now
That our love cannot survive.

If only I had described to you
The joy you brought to me,
Instead of bringing you complaints,
You wouldn't have set me free.

If I had touched you, kissed you, Love,
If I had loved you stronger,
If I had appreciated you,
We would have lasted longer.

If I had often said to you,
"It's you whom I adore,"
Perhaps you'd still be with me now,
If I had told you more.

If only I had treated you
As if we were best friends,
I wouldn't be alone in grief,
As our faded love finally ends.

If only I didn't have to say,
"If only, my love, if only,"
I wouldn't be all by myself
So sorry, sad and lonely.

By Joanna Fuchs

Idle Dreams

In idle dreams of long ago,
I imagined my true love;
A perfect match, a soul mate,
An angel from above.

Now you're here, and now I know
Our love will stay and thrive and grow.

By Joanna Fuchs

My Perfect Refuge

When life is cold,
I wrap myself in your warmth,
nestled in your love,
my perfect refuge.

By Joanna Fuchs

I Never Knew

I never knew about happiness;
I didn't think dreams came true;
I couldn't believe in love,
Until I finally met you.

By Joanna Fuchs

Every Thought of You

Each thought of you fills me with sweet emotion;
I give to you my deep, complete devotion.
All my fondest wishes you fulfill;
I love you totally, and I always will.

By Joanna Fuchs

It's You

Of everything I know and love and treasure,
It's you, my love, who gives me perfect pleasure.
I love your way with me, your touch, your kiss;
To be with you is happiness and bliss.

By Joanna Fuchs

My Everything

When all goes wrong, and my life runs amok,
I think of you, and I get unstuck;
In the midst of chaos, you make my heart sing;
You're my peace, my happiness, my everything.

By Joanna Fuchs

You're Perfect

Your femininity/masculinity attracts me;
Your steady strength supports me;
Your tenderness sustains me;
You're the perfect love for me.

By Joanna Fuchs

You Win

It's crazy, but you're all I want and need;
You win; I'm yours forever; I concede.

By Joanna Fuchs

I Always Will

I loved you then,
And I love you still;
I adore you now,
And I always will.

By Joanna Fuchs

Mother Poems

A Sonnet for My Incomparable Mother

I often contemplate my childhood, Mom.
I am a mother now, and so I know
Hard work is mixed together with the fun;
You learned that when you raised me long ago.

I think of all the things you gave to me:
Sacrifice, devotion, love and tears,
Your heart, your mind, your energy and soul--
All these you spent on me throughout the years.

You loved me with a never-failing love;
You gave me strength and sweet security,
And then you did the hardest thing of all:
You let me separate and set me free.

Every day, I try my best to be
A mother like the mom you were to me.

By Joanna Fuchs

You Let Me Know You Love Me

You let me know you love me
In so many different ways.
You make me feel important
With encouragement and praise.

You're always there when I need you
To comfort and to care.
I know I'm in your thoughts;
Your love follows me everywhere.

Thank you for all you've done
And given so generously.
I love you, my wonderful mother;
You're a heaven-sent blessing to me.

By Joanna Fuchs

Nobody's Like You, Mom

Nobody's quite like you, Mom.
You're special in every way.
You cheer me up, you fill my cup
With tenderness, come what may.

Nobody loves me like you, Mom.
No matter what I do,
Good or bad, happy or sad,
You support me; you always come through.

Nobody's equal to you, Mom.
With you in my life, I'm blessed.
I love you so, and I want you to know
I think you're the very best!

By Joanna Fuchs

Super Mom

Mom, you're a wonderful mother,
So gentle, yet so strong.
The many ways you show you care
Always make me feel I belong.

You're patient when I'm foolish;
You give guidance when I ask;
It seems you can do most anything;
You're the master of every task.

You're a dependable source of comfort;
You're my cushion when I fall.
You help in times of trouble;
You support me whenever I call.

I love you more than you know;
You have my total respect.
If I had my choice of mothers,
You'd be the one I'd select!

By Joanna Fuchs

Everything Mom

How did you find the energy, Mom
To do all the things you did,
To be teacher, nurse and counselor
To me, when I was a kid.

How did you do it all, Mom,
Be a chauffeur, cook and friend,
Yet find time to be a playmate,
I just can't comprehend.

I see now it was love, Mom
That made you come whenever I'd call,
Your inexhaustible love, Mom
And I thank you for it all.

By Joanna Fuchs

Without You

Mom, without you, there would be no me.
Your love, your attention, your guidance,
have made me who I am.
Without you, I would be lost,
wandering aimlessly,
without direction or purpose.
You showed me the way
to serve, to accomplish, to persevere.
Without you, there would be an empty space
I could never fill, no matter how I tried.
Instead, because of you,
I have joy, contentment, satisfaction and peace.
Thank you, mom.
I have always loved you
and I always will.

By Joanna Fuchs

What "Mother" Means

"Mother" is such a simple word,
But to me there's meaning seldom heard.

For everything I am today,
My mother's love showed me the way.

I'll love my mother all my days,
For enriching my life in so many ways.
She set me straight and then set me free,
And that's what the word "mother" means to me.

By Karl Fuchs

My Miracle Mother

Mom, I look at you
and see a walking miracle.
Your unfailing love without limit,
your ability to soothe my every hurt,
the way you are on duty, unselfishly,
every hour, every day,
makes me so grateful
that I am yours, and you are mine.
With open arms and open heart,
with enduring patience and inner strength,
you gave so much for me,
sometimes at your expense.
You are my teacher,
my comforter, my encourager,
appreciating all, forgiving all.
Sometimes I took you for granted, Mom,
but I don't now, and I never will again.
I know that everything I am today
relates to you and your loving care.
I gaze in wonder
as I watch you being you—
my miracle, my mother.

By Joanna Fuchs

I Learned From You

I learned about love from you,
Watching your caring ways.
I learned about joy from you
In fun-filled yesterdays.

From you I learned forgiving
Of faults both big and small.
I learned what I know about living
From you, as you gave life your all.

The example you set is still with me
I'd never want any other.
I'm thankful for all that you taught me,
And I'm blessed to call you "Mother."

By Joanna Fuchs

A Thousand Thanks

Mother's Day brings to mind
The thousands of things you did for me
that helped make me happier,
stronger and wiser,
because I had you as a role model.

I'm grateful for all the times
you healed my hurts
and calmed my fears,
so that I could face the world
feeling safe and secure.

I'm thankful for all you showed me
about how to love and give--
lessons that now bring
so many blessings to me
each and every day.

Your sacrifices and unselfishness
did not go unnoticed, Mom.
I admire you, I respect you,
I love you.
And I'm so glad you're my mother!

By Joanna Fuchs

Extra Special Mom

Mom, you've always been the best
A better mom than all the rest.
I'm thankful for all the things you do
I'm glad my mom is extra special you!

On Mother's Day, I want you to know
You're the greatest mom, and I love you so.
There's one more thing I want to say:
I wish you Happy Mother's Day!

By Joanna Fuchs

Best Mom Award

For all the things I didn't say,
About how I felt along the way--
For the love you gave, and the work you've done,
Here's appreciation from your admiring son.

You cared for me as a little tot,
When all I did was cry a lot,
And as I grew your work did too--
I ran and fell and got black and blue.

I grew some more and it didn't stop.
Now you had to become a cop,
To worry about mistakes I'd make;
You kept me in line for my own sake.

I got older, and the story repeated;
You were always there whenever I needed.
You guided me and wished me the best,
I became wiser and knew I was blessed.

So, for all the times I didn't say,
The love I felt for you each day,
Mom, read this so you can always see
Just how much you mean to me.

By Karl Fuchs

Daughter of My Heart

You turned out even better
Than I often dreamed you'd be;
You're more than I had hoped for;
You're a sweet reward to me.

You grew up to be a mother
Full of wisdom, warmth and love,
A good and fine role model,
A blessing from above.

I couldn't be any prouder
Than I am today of you;
You're my daughter and my friend,
And a wonderful person, too.

You have my love forever;
I adored you from the start;
It's a privilege to be your mother,
Dear daughter of my heart.

By Joanna Fuchs

Mother-In-Law Poem

Star Mother-In-Law

Some mother-in-laws are possessive;
Their child they still want to own.
My mother-in-law's love is like sunlight;
On both of us it shone.

Some mother-in-laws put you down;
They think you're not good enough.
My mother-in-law shows approval,
Affection, and other good stuff.

Some mother-in-laws interfere;
They think that they know best.
My mother-in-law lets us be;
She's better than the rest.

And so I just want to thank you
For being the person you are;
You've made everything so easy;
As a mother-in-law, you're a star!

By Joanna Fuchs

Mother's Day Poems From Children

I'm Happy You're My Mom

I'm happy you're my mom,
'Cause you take good care of me.
You love me and you show it,
So I'm as happy as can be!

I love you very much,
And so I want to say,
Thank you for all you do,
And Happy Mother's Day!

By Joanna Fuchs

Mommy, I Love You

Mommy, I know you love me
By the way you show you care.
You hug me and talk to me softly;
When I need you, you're always there.

Mommy, I'll love you always;
From my heart, I want to say,
I'm so glad you are my mommy;
Happy Mother's Day!

By Joanna Fuchs

Grandma Mother's Day Poem

Wonderful Grandma

Grandma, you're so wonderful,
On Mother's Day I think of you--
The unconditional love you give
The sweet and generous things you do.

You've made a difference in my life;
I love you more than I can say.
That's why I give this poem to you,
To wish you "Happy Mother's Day!"

By Joanna Fuchs

Wife Mother's Day Poem

Happy Mother's Day To My Wife

On Mother's day, I want to wish
Happy Mother's Day to my wonderful wife;
My friend, my love, a terrific mom,
You bring so much happiness into my life.

You're everything to this family;
I appreciate you, and I want to say,
The day we met, I was truly blessed.
Happy, Happy Mother's Day!

By Joanna Fuchs

Sister Mother's Day Poem

Mother's Day Poem For Sister

I've been watching you be a mother, Sis,
And I just want you to know,
I admire you and respect you, because
As a mom, you are a pro!

I love you, Sis, and now I see
You're amazing in every way;
You're my sister, a mom and a friend as well;
Happy Mother's Day!

By Joanna Fuchs

Aunt Mother's Day Poem

Aunt Mother's Day Poem

Dear Aunt, I wish I could express
All the things you mean to me;
Your love and support have helped so much;
I hope I can make you see…

That I cherish and treasure the things you do;
You and I have a special connection;
So on Mother's Day and every day,
You have my very deep affection.

By Joanna Fuchs

Friend Mother's Day Poem

Mother's Day Poem For a Friend

I'm proud to have you as my friend,
A wonderful friend for me;
You're also a great mother, too;
I watch you admiringly.

Observing you, I often think
How blessed the world is now
To have you in it, friend and mom,
Happy Mother's Day; take a bow!

By Joanna Fuchs

Step Mother Poem

I'm so blessed that you're my step mom;
Let me tell you how I feel:
The deep affection I have for you
Is honest, true and real.

On Mother's Day, I'm really glad
I'm able to convey
How glad I am you're in my life;
Happy Mother's Day!

By Joanna Fuchs

Mother's Day Songs

Mother Is The Best

(To the tune of "Row, Row, Row Your Boat")

My mom is really great;
She's sweet as she can be;
When I need some help, I know
She's always there for me.

Mom loves me all the time,
Even when I'm a pest;
She always takes good care of me;
My mother is the best.

By Joanna Fuchs

Love Is A Mother's Gift

(To the tune of "Green Sleeves")

When God made mothers, He took great care
To fill their hearts with love so rare.
Their children are their greatest prize;
You can see the great love in your mother's eyes.

Love, love is a mother's gift
To their precious children, their hearts to lift.
Warm, tender and giving love
That grows them up healthy and happy.

Thank you, mother for all you give
To help me grow and to help me live.
I will love you forevermore,
My mother, my mom, whom I adore.

(Repeat second verse)

By Joanna Fuchs

Memorial Mother Poem

Mother's Day Poem For A Deceased Mother

Mom, we miss you so very much
On every Mother's Day;
And not just then, but every minute,
Since you went away.

You were the center of our lives
Before your soul passed on;
It's just so hard for us to believe
That you are really gone.

But we celebrate the life you lived
And all the things you gave us;
Our wonderful memories, Mom, of you
Are the things that will comfort and save us.

Please think of us, as we think of you
With hearts so full of love;
We're looking up at you, sweet Mom,
As you look at us from above.

By Joanna Fuchs

The Fruit of the Spirit

My mother is a Christian,
In every important way;
The fruit of the Holy Spirit
Is displayed in her every day.

My mother is filled with kindness,
With love and joy and peace;
Her patience and her goodness
Inspire, and never cease.

She follows our Lord Jesus
With faithfulness, and more;
She's gentle and has self control,
She knows what prayer is for.

Thanks, Mom, for being a Christian,
And showing me how to be;
I'll follow your example
For all eternity.

By Joanna Fuchs

Mother Prayer

Mother Prayer

Dear Lord,
today we pray for mothers--
our own mothers, and mothers everywhere,
who have made such a major contribution
to the good qualities we have,
sometimes through genetics,
more often through great effort and patient instruction,
and who have done their best
to gently polish away our rough edges.
Lord, please bless our mothers
for the endless hours of time they spent
and the boundless energy they invested in us.
Bless our mothers for their sacrifices on our behalf

as they often gave up or deferred their own dreams
so that we could have ours.
Bless our mothers for always being there for us,
for being the person we know we can turn to
when we need comfort, encouragement, or just a hug.
Bless our mothers for making a home for us
where we could feel safe, where we felt we belonged.
Most of all, Lord,
bless our mothers for their unconditional love,
for loving us no matter what,
and for frequently showing love
in ways that make us feel valued and cherished.
Lord, please bless our mothers mightily.
Strengthen them, soothe them,
wrap them in Your infinite love
and shower them with blessings
too numerous to count, too magnificent to describe.
We love them, admire them, respect them,
and we wish that You would give them back
many times the good they gave to us.
In Jesus' name we pray; Amen.

By Joanna Fuchs

New Year Poems

New Year's Reflections

Looking back on the months gone by,
As a new year starts and an old one ends,
We contemplate what brought us joy,
And we think of our loved ones and our friends.

Recalling all the happy times,
Remembering how they enriched our lives,
We reflect upon who really counts,
As the fresh and bright new year arrives.

And when we ponder those who do,
We immediately think of you.

By Joanna Fuchs

Happy New Year Wish

My Happy New Year wish for you
Is for your best year yet,
A year where life is peaceful,
And what you want, you get.

A year in which you cherish
The past year's memories,
And live your life each new day
Full of bright expectancies.

I wish for you a holiday
With happiness galore;
And when it's done, I wish you
Happy New Year, and many more.

By Joanna Fuchs

Happy New Year To You

Happy New Year to you!
May every great new day
Bring you sweet surprises--
A happiness buffet.

Happy New Year to you,
And when the new year's done,
May the next year be even better,
Full of pleasure, joy and fun.

By Joanna Fuchs

In The New Year

In the New Year,
we wish you the best year you've ever had,
and that each New Year
will be better than the last.
May you realize your fondest dreams
and take time to recognize and enjoy
each and every blessing.

By Joanna Fuchs

Pieces of Time

New years come and new years go,
Pieces of time all in a row.
As we live our life, each second and minute,
We know we're privileged to have you in it.
Our appreciation never ends
For our greatest blessings: our family and friends.

By Joanna Fuchs

People Like You

A brand new year!
A clean slate on which to write
our hopes and dreams.
This year:

Less time and energy on things;
More time and energy on people.
All of life's best rewards,
deepest and finest feelings,
greatest satisfactions,
Come from people--
People like you.

By Joanna Fuchs

New Year's Eve Party Poems

Bring Your Awesome Self

The New Year's rolling in;
We're planning quite a bash.
We need to have you here.
So it will be a smash!

We really want to see you;
We hope that you can make it.
So help us make our party fun,
Or we might have to fake it!

Just bring your awesome self
And what you want to drink.
And we'll provide the other stuff,
Including the kitchen sink!

When you let us know you'll come,
We'll smile and shout "Whoopee!"
So sit right down and phone/write us
With your kind R.S.V.P!

By Joanna Fuchs

The New Year's Eve Party

The new year is coming; the party is near.
I'm sure looking forward to lots of good cheer.
I'll be all dressed up in my snazziest best,
So I won't disappear in the crowd, like the rest.

I rap on the door, and it opens to screams;
There are several guys hanging from high ceiling beams.
The guy in the lampshade looks ready to go,
As the girl on his shoulders shouts, "Giddy up Joe!"

I walk right on in to be one of the throng,
And they yell out my name, while they bang a brass gong.
We laugh and we frolic, we dance and we sing,
(Is that my grandmother out there on the swing?)

This party is great, and the New Year looks bright.
Well, that's how I dreamed it, while sleeping last night.
I'm thinking about you and wish you were here,
So I'm sending this poem to say Happy New Year!

By Karl and Joanna Fuchs

Happy New Year Song

(To the tune of Beethoven's "Ode to Joy")

To the New Year

Happy New Year, Happy New Year,
Family, friends and colleagues, too.
May this new year be your best yet,
Happiness the whole year through.

Let's all join to lift our glasses
In a toast to everyone.
To the old year now behind us,
To the new year, just begun.

(Repeat first verse)

By Joanna Fuchs

The Gift of a New Year (Toast)

Here's to the year
that's almost past its expiration date—(year).
We all had some surprises, didn't we?
Some good, some distressing.
Let's use everything we got from our experiences,
everything we learned,
to enrich the new year.

Here's to the new year, (year),
a gift we haven't opened yet.
May its bright, shiny package
contain even more than we hope for.

And even while we're delighting in new treasures,
let's appreciate fully what we already have—
the blessings we take for granted.
Make a list, and check it twice.

And here's to all you wonderful people
(wave glass around to encompass the whole group)
who are putting up with my toast;
I hope in the new year
you see yourselves the way I see you:
intelligent, interesting, and likable.

(Raise glass) To (year):
May it give a whole new meaning
to the phrase, "the good life."

By Joanna Fuchs

Fulfillment in the New Year (Toast)

Here's to the outgoing year, (year):
May the good times live on in our memories,
and may we learn lessons from the troubling times
that will make us stronger and better than ever.

Here's to (year):
For each and every one of you,

may it be filled with significant steps
toward the fulfillment of your fondest wishes.

In this coming new year,
let us focus on our goals and work toward our dreams,
and yet (smile)
let's all try to go with the flow a little more
and stress a little less.

And most important,
(wave glass around to encompass the whole group)
here's to all of you.
Appreciate yourselves and each other in the new year
as I appreciate all of you now.
Let's focus on each other's good points
and choose to overlook minor annoyances
to create mutual happiness and contentment in (year).

Here's to (year) (raise glass): Enjoy the journey!

By Joanna Fuchs

New Year Toast

Here's to the new year...
May it bring more joy and success
and less grief and regret.

To our dreams...
May we never stop believing in them
and taking the actions that will make them a reality.

To our friends, loved ones, associates (or colleagues)...
May we take the time to let them know
how much it means to us
to have them in our lives.

Let us encourage more and criticize less,
give more and need less.
And whenever we can,
let us create harmony and peace.

To new beginnings...
Let us start fresh, right now,

to make this the very best year ever.
A very Happy New Year to all of us!

By Joanna Fuchs

New Year's Resolution Poems

New Year's Reality Check

Another year, another chance
To start our lives anew;
This time we'll leap old barriers
To have a real breakthrough.

We'll take one little step
And then we'll take one more,
Our unlimited potential
We'll totally explore.

We'll show off all our talents;
Everyone will be inspired;
(Whew! While I'm writing this,
I'm getting very tired.)

We'll give up all bad habits;
We'll read and learn a lot,
All our goals will be accomplished,
Sigh...or maybe not.

By Joanna Fuchs

New Year's Resolutions

Each year I resolve with the strongest intent
To be better this year than the last.
And I work very hard; the rules hardly get bent,
But this discipline gets old so fast!

But with this new year I just know I'll win out,
Just watch how I do and you'll see!
I'm not going to have yet another blowout;
I'll be good as I know I can be.

But, if wicked things beckon, and I'm not so strong,
If I weaken and fall on my ast,
I'll be thankful again that you'll help me along
As you have during all new years past.

By Karl and Joanna Fuchs

Christian New Year's Resolutions

How can I use the New Year
To better serve my Lord?
I'll read my Bible every day,
And be more in accord.

I'll find new ways to serve others;
I'll love my neighbor, too.
I'll focus on "give" instead of "get"
In everything I do.

I'll forgive the people I'm mad at;
Angry feelings I'll discard;
I'll try to love my enemies,
Even though it's hard.

In the new year, I'll lift people up,
Instead of putting them down.
I'll fill my heart with love and joy,
And never wear a frown.

I'll let go of my worries;
I'll put it all in His hands;
I'll repent and try to sin less,
And obey all His commands.

These New Year's resolutions
Are difficult, at best,
But there's something I can do each day
That will put my soul at rest:

I'll love my Lord with all my heart,
With all my mind and soul,
And if I do that essential thing,
All the rest will be in control.

By Joanna Fuchs

Guide Us Each New Day

Dear Lord,
In the new year, we pray
that You will guide us each new day
in paths that are pleasing to You.
Lord, the new year gives us another chance
to rededicate our lives to You,
to study Your Word
so that we know right from wrong
and to act in accordance with Your commands.
Thank You for the sense of
direction, purpose and peace we get
from aligning our lives with Your Holy will.
We pray for the strength and the will to obey You
each and every day of the new year,
and when we fail, we pray for Your mercy,
Your compassion, Your grace and Your love.
Help us in the new year to be Your faithful servants.
In Jesus' name we pray, Amen.

By Joanna Fuchs

PATRIOTIC POEMS

They Did Their Share

On Veteran's Day we honor
Soldiers who protect our nation.
For their service as our warriors,
They deserve our admiration.

Some of them were drafted;
Some were volunteers;
For some it was just yesterday;
For some it's been many years;

In the jungle or the desert,
On land or on the sea,
They did whatever was assigned
To produce a victory.

Some came back; some didn't;
They defended us everywhere.
Some saw combat; some rode a desk;
All of them did their share.

No matter what the duty,
For low pay and little glory,
These soldiers gave up normal lives,
For duties mundane and gory.

Let every veteran be honored;
Don't let politics get in the way;
Without them, freedom would have died;
What they did, we can't repay.

We owe so much to them,
Who kept us safe from terror,
So when we see a uniform,
Let's say "thank you" to every wearer.

By Joanna Fuchs

The Noble and the Brave

When America had an urgent need,
These brave ones raised a hand;
No hesitation held them back;
They were proud to take a stand.

They left their friends and family;
They gave up normal life;
To serve their country and their God,
They plowed into the strife.

They fought for freedom and for peace
On strange and foreign shores;
Some lost new friends; some lost their lives
In long and brutal wars.

Other veterans answered a call
To support the ones who fought;
Their country had requirements for
The essential skills they brought.

We salute every one of them,
The noble and the brave,
The ones still with us here today,
And those who rest in a grave.

So here's to our country's heroes;
They're a cut above the rest;
Let's give the honor that is due
To our country's very best.

By Joanna Fuchs

The Best on Earth

If someone has done military service,
They earn the title "veteran," and more;
They earn our deep respect and admiration;
That they are special no one can ignore.

They sacrificed the comforts we enjoy;
The list is long of all the things they gave;
Our veterans are extraordinary people;
They're loyal, dedicated, true and brave.

When terror and invasion were real threats,
They showed us they could handle any storm.
We owe our freedoms and our very lives
To our veterans, who served in uniform.

Our veterans should be celebrities;
They're exceptional; no other group compares.
We're grateful for the many things they've done;
They're always in our hearts and in our prayers.

We owe our veterans support and friendship;
Let no one ever question what they're worth.
These men and women served us and our country;
Our veterans--the very best on earth.

By Joanna Fuchs

Take A Moment To Thank A Veteran

When you see someone in a uniform,
Someone who serves us all,
Doing military duty,
Answering their country's call,

Take a moment to thank them
For protecting what you hold dear;
Tell them you are proud of them;
Make it very clear.

Just tap them on the shoulder,
Give a smile, and say,
"Thanks for what you're doing;
To keep us safe in the USA!"

By Joanna Fuchs

Veteran's Day Prayer

Bless Them Abundantly

Dear Lord,
Today we honor our veterans,
worthy men and women
who gave their best
when they were called upon
to serve and protect their country.
We pray that you will bless them, Lord,
for their unselfish service
in the continual struggle
to preserve our freedoms, our safety,
and our country's heritage, for all of us.
Bless them abundantly
for the hardships they faced,
the sacrifices they made,
for their many different contributions
to America's victories
over tyranny and oppression.
We respect them, thank them,
we honor them, we are proud of them,
and we pray that you will watch over
these special people
and bless them with peace and happiness.
In Jesus' name we pray; Amen.

By Joanna Fuchs

Armed Forces Day Poem

Honor Our Military

Let's honor our military,
The men and women who serve,
Whose dedication to our country
Does not falter, halt or swerve.

Let's respect them for their courage;
They're ready to do what's right,
To keep America safe,
So we can sleep better at night.

162

Let's support and defend our soldiers,
Whose hardships are brutal and cruel,
Whose discipline we can't imagine,
Who follow each order and rule.

Here's to those who choose to be warriors
And their helpers good and true;
They're fighting for American values;
They're fighting for me and you.

By Joanna Fuchs

Memorial Day Poems

The Ultimate Sacrifice

We set aside Memorial Day
Each and every year
To honor those who gave their lives,
Defending what we hold dear.

In all the dark and deadly wars,
Their graves prove and remind us,
Our brave Americans gave their all
To put danger far behind us.

They made the ultimate sacrifice
Fighting for the American way;
We admire them and respect them
On every Memorial Day.

By Joanna Fuchs

In Loving Memory

On every soldier's tombstone
should be a message of honor, respect and love:
"In loving memory
of one who loved his country,
who fought against evil
to preserve what is right and true and good.

In loving memory
of one who is a cut above the rest of us,
who had the surpassing courage,
the uncommon strength,
to do whatever had to be done,
persevering through hardship and pain.
In loving memory
of one who was brave enough
to give his life, his all,
so that those he cared about
would remain safe and free.
In loving memory
of a unique and treasured soldier
who will never be forgotten."

By Joanna Fuchs

Flag Day Poem

Our Flag Flies High

The U.S. flag is a symbol
Of what Americans treasure;
It represents the values
We cherish beyond measure.

Our flag flies high for freedom,
For legal equality,
For Constitutional rights,
And justice for you and me.

Our flag flies high for bravery,
The courage it takes to fight
And even give our lives
For what we know is right.

Our flag flies high for compassion;
We quickly help those in need;
When there's a need for service,
Americans take the lead.

The American flag is an icon,
Representing the American way;

Our hearts swell with emotion,
When we see it ripple and sway.

By Joanna Fuchs

Fourth of July Poem

Free In The USA

On the Fourth of July, I raised the flag,
As I spoke with love and pride:
"I'm blessed to be an American," I said,
To two friends who stood by my side.

One was my neighbor, who lives next door,
He's a citizen, like me.
The other, a visitor from a hard, oppressed land,
Far across the sea.

"My flag stays in its box this year,"
Said my neighbor, boiling mad.
"The terrible shape this country's in,
The future looks nothing but bad.

"Taxes, scandal, indifference and crime,
On our land like a giant stain."
My visitor said, "We have all that, and worse,
But it's against the law to complain."

My neighbor looked startled, but not subdued;
Then he started in on the Press:
"There's nothing but bad news; the headlines are bleak."
(It gets me down, too, I confess.)

"Our news is all good," said my visitor.
"It's just how you'd like to be.
We know what our government wants us to know;
Our press is controlled, you see."

My neighbor spun 'round and marched toward his house,
And here is the end to my story:
The next time we saw him, he was out in his yard,
Proudly raising Old Glory.

By Joanna Fuchs

Soldier's Prayer

Wrap Your Arms Around Me

Lord, wrap Your arms around me
In this hostile, brutal place;
Let me draw peace and comfort
From Your restful, sweet embrace.

Help me do my duty
To uphold what is right;
Give me strength and courage
Each day and every night.

Lord, hear this soldier's prayer
To You in heaven above;
Protect me with Your power,
And sustain me with Your love.

By Joanna Fuchs

War Poems

I Miss You

I miss you in the morning,
I miss you late at night,
But I know what you are doing
Is good and just and right.

You're always in my thoughts;
I hope that you can see
I'm proud of you for serving
Our country, God, and me.

And when you're home again
I won't miss you anymore,
But I'll always admire your courage
For fighting in this war.

By Joanna Fuchs

The Tyrants

The tyrants are on the loose again;
They hate all but their own.
They give their lives to kill us,
To scatter our blood and bone.

They care not whom they murder,
Whether woman, man or child;
Their minds are full of fury;
Their sickness has gone wild.

To rule the world with violence
Is their one and only goal;
Terror is their method;
They want complete control.

We've seen it all before,
And we could not let it be;
We gave our lives for freedom,
For the world, and for you and me.

We fight all forms of oppression,
Helping victims far and near,
To keep the world from chaos,
To protect what we hold dear.

America's the only country
That gives with its whole heart,
And asks so very little;
We always do our part.

So let's unite again
To subdue our newest foe,
Whatever we must do,
Wherever we must go.

Let's show the world once more
That America is blessed
With people who are heroes,
Who meet each and every test.

By Joanna Fuchs

Make War, Not Love

Except for those who make the guns
And profit from each bomb and plane,
No one wants war; we all want peace.
"Bring them home!" people complain.

There are better ways to solve all this;
We'll get together and negotiate;
With diplomacy, we'll calm them down;
With loving hearts we'll end the hate.

But loving hearts don't understand
That demented tyrants want it all.
No talk, no love will change their minds;
Only war will cause their fall.

Hitler, Stalin, Pol Pot, too,
Total power was their goal.
Saddam Hussein, Amin, and more,
Ignored the talk, and gained control.

Despicable, depraved and more,
With viciousness, they kill their own.
So we send our soldiers off to hell
To keep freedom as our cornerstone.

Was 9/11 not enough
To show us just how far they'll go?
Will we acquiesce to terrorists,
These devils, the lowest of the low?

Reluctantly, we have to fight;
So while pundits chatter and discuss,
We'll use our might to take them out,
To keep the thugs from killing us.

By Joanna Fuchs

SYMPATHY POEMS

General Sympathy Poems

Reaching Out

My heart is reaching out to you,
For what you're going through;
I'm thinking of you frequently
And praying for you, too.

If there's something I can do,
Anything at all,
Think of me thinking of you,
And don't hesitate to call.

By Joanna Fuchs

After They Are Gone

When someone we love passes away,
We ache, but we go on;
Our dear departed would want us to heal,
After they are gone.

Grief is a normal way to mend
The anguish and pain in our hearts;
We need time to remember and time to mourn,
Before the recovery starts.

Let's draw together to recuperate,
As we go through this period of sorrow;
Let's help each other, with tender care
To find a brighter tomorrow.

By Joanna Fuchs

If We Could Bring You Back Again

If we could bring you back again,
For one more hour or day,
We'd express all our unspoken love;
We'd have countless things to say.

If we could bring you back again,
We'd say we treasured you,
And that your presence in our lives
Meant more than we ever knew.

If we could bring you back again,
To tell you what we should,
You'd know how much we miss you now,
And if we could, we would.

By Joanna Fuchs

A Better Place

She's in a better place right now
Than she's ever been before;
All pain is gone; she's now at rest;
Nothing troubles her anymore.

It's we who feel the burden of
Our sadness and our grief;.
We have to cry, to mourn our loss,
Before we get relief.

We know we'll reconnect with her
At the end of each life's road;
We'll see her cherished face again
When we release our earthly load.

By Joanna Fuchs

Sending Sympathy

I'm so sorry to hear of your recent loss;
I'm sending my sympathy;
If you need someone to help you now,
Please, friend, call on me.

By Joanna Fuchs

No One Can Know

No one can know just what you've lost;
No one can understand the cost;
But when you feel your energy drain,
Please count on us to help ease your pain.

Let us help you cope with grief;
We hope with time you'll feel relief.
We can't replace the one who's gone,
But let our concern help you carry on.

By Karl and Joanna Fuchs

We're With You

When you miss her,
we're with you in spirit,
wondering how you feel,
hoping you're coping,
and getting a little better each day.
We understand. We care.
When you're grieving,
we're beside you,
in our hearts, in our thoughts,
we're sending you sympathy,
encouragement, affection,
and strength to carry on with life.
He would want it that way.

By Joanna Fuchs

Just Call On Me

I can't comprehend just how sad you must feel
For the loss of someone you love.
This sorrowful time must still feel unreal
And you're looking for strength from above.

I hope, from my heart, that your pain will decrease,
That your spirit will gain strength again,
And I pray that your faith will create inner peace
And that God will send blessings--Amen.

171

Till then, if you need me to lighten your load,
I'm waiting to come to your aid.
Just call on me, and I'll walk down that road,
Until the dark times start to fade.

By Karl Fuchs

Pet Sympathy Poem

Sweet Presence

Today I'm often thinking of you,
And the loss of your special friend.
Those who have never had a pet
Cannot possibly comprehend.

A pet gives unconditional love
Nothing else can quite replace;
A sweet presence with its furry warmth,
That loveable, one-of-a-kind face.

You gave your pet a happy life,
With affection true and real;
I'm hoping you'll recover soon
So your heart will mend and heal.

By Joanna Fuchs

TEACHER POEMS

The Teacher Gets A+

I look forward to your class
When I come to school.
You're an awesome teacher;
I think you're very cool.

You're smart and fair and friendly;
You're helping all of us.
And if I got to grade you,
From me you'd get A+!

By Joanna Fuchs

Number One Teacher

I'm happy that you're my teacher;
I enjoy each lesson you teach.
As my role model you inspire me
To dream and to work and to reach.

With your kindness you get my attention;
Every day you are planting a seed
Of curiosity and motivation
To know and to grow and succeed.

You help me fulfill my potential;
I'm thankful for all that you've done.
I admire you each day, and I just want to say,
As a teacher, you're number one!

By Joanna Fuchs

A Teacher for All Seasons

A teacher is like Spring,
Who nurtures new green sprouts,
Encourages and leads them,
Whenever they have doubts.

A teacher is like Summer,
Whose sunny temperament
Makes studying a pleasure,
Preventing discontent.

A teacher is like Fall,
With methods crisp and clear,
Lessons of bright colors
And a happy atmosphere.

A teacher is like Winter,
While it's snowing hard outside,
Keeping students comfortable,
As a warm and helpful guide.

Teacher, you do all these things,
With a pleasant attitude;
You're a teacher for all seasons,
And you have my gratitude!

By Joanna Fuchs

If I Could Teach You, Teacher

If I could teach you, teacher,
I'd teach you how much more
you have accomplished
than you think you have.
I'd show you the seeds
you planted years ago
that are now coming into bloom.
I'd reveal to you the young minds
that have expanded under your care,
the hearts that are serving others
because they had you as a role model.
If I could teach you, teacher,
I'd show you the positive effect

you have had on me and my life.
Your homework is
to know your value to the world,
to acknowledge it, to believe it.
Thank you, teacher.

By Joanna Fuchs

Sonnet For An Unforgettable Teacher

When I began your class I think I knew
The kind of challenges you'd make me face.
You gave me motivation to pursue
The best, and to reject the commonplace.

Your thinking really opened up my mind.
With wisdom, style and grace, you made me see,
That what I'd choose to seek, I'd surely find;
You shook me out of my complacency.

I thank you now for everything you've done;
What you have taught me I will not outgrow.
Your kind attention touched my mind and heart;
In many ways that you will never know.

I will remember you my whole life through;
I wish that all my teachers were like you.

By Joanna Fuchs

The Best Teachers

Teachers open up young minds,
showing them the wonders of the intellect
and the miracle of being able to think for themselves.
A teacher exercises the mental muscles of students,
stretching and strengthening,
so they can make challenging decisions,
find their way in the world,
and become independent.
The best teachers care enough

to gently push and prod students to do their best
and fulfill their potential.
You are one of those.
Thank you.

By Joanna Fuchs

Star Teacher

I always love your class;
Your teaching helps me see,
That to have a happy life,
Learning is the key.

You understand your students;
You're sensitive and smart.
You're a skillful teacher;
I knew it from the start.

I'm grateful for your wisdom
For the teacher that you are;
You're a very good person,
And as a teacher, you're a star!

By Joanna Fuchs

The Most Admired Teacher

The most admired teacher
Would be caring, kind and smart.
She'd always have her students'
Best interests in her heart.

She'd help us love to learn;
Her lessons would be clear;
She'd motivate with praise,
And always be sincere.

She'd be upbeat and supportive,
And a great role model too.
She'd be the perfect teacher;
She'd be just like you!

By Joanna Fuchs

I'll Remember You Always

Rarely does someone
get to influence a person's life
in a positive way for a lifetime,
as a teacher can,
fostering optimism and confidence,
providing knowledge that leads to success,
and being a good role model,
as you have,
and you are,
and you will...
forever.
I'll remember you always.
Thank you.

By Joanna Fuchs

Thank You, Teacher

Thank you, skillful teacher,
For teaching me to be
A stronger, smarter person,
Academically.

Thank you, favorite teacher
For acting like a friend,
And taking time to show me,
Lessons hard to comprehend.

Thank you for your caring
And lots of other stuff;
For all the things you gave me,
I can't thank you enough.

By Joanna Fuchs

Special Teacher

Thank you special teacher
For helping me to know
The things I need to learn
To live my life and grow.

I feel good with you because
Your teaching makes me see,
If I work at it, I can do it.
Thanks for showing me!

By Joanna Fuchs

Lessons Are Fun

I'm happy you're my teacher;
Thanks for all you do.
You make learning easy;
Your lessons are fun, too!

By Joanna Fuchs

We'll Remember You

Thank you teacher for helping us
To learn what we need to know
We'll all remember you
No matter where we go.

Thank you, teacher, for always being
So nice and kind and good;
We like you so much, teacher,
We'd stay here if we could!

By Joanna Fuchs

Poem From Teacher To Student

Students Like You

With students like you, teaching is easy
I look forward to each day;
Your wondering minds keep me on my toes;
You make teaching more like play.

Students like you make teaching rewarding;
When I go home, I'm content;
You pay attention, you learn—giving me
A sense of accomplishment.

Thank you for being the way you are,
For making my job so much fun.
I'll remember how good you made me feel,
Even when my teaching is done.

By Joanna Fuchs

Sunday School Teacher Poem

Thank You, Sunday School Teacher

Thank you Sunday school teacher
For opening my eyes
To the Bible and to Jesus,
Life's most precious prize.

Thank you special teacher
For opening my mind
To God and the Holy Spirit,
And for answers you help me find.

Thank you Sunday school teacher
For opening my heart
To eternal life through salvation,
The precious lessons you impart.

Thank you, cherished teacher,
For giving me advice
So that I can know the Lord
And be with Him in paradise.

By Joanna Fuchs

Teacher Prayer

Dear Lord, bless these teachers mightily
as they seek to teach, enrich and guide
Your precious children.
Grant them abundant resources to do their job,
intelligence, wisdom, sensitivity, kindness,
and the material things that make it possible
to turn some of these tender green plants
into the strong, stable trees that will lead our nation,
to transform some of these buds into brilliant flowers
that will bring light, color and happiness
to all who encounter them,
and to give every one of them the tools
to be creative, and productive and to develop
their own kind of success in the world.
Lord, wrap Your loving arms around these teachers
who give so much of themselves to grow our youth
into creative, responsible adults.
We pray that You will immerse them
in your boundless, transcendent love.
We pray that You will strengthen and soothe them
when they need Your extra attention, Your extra care.
We love, respect and admire these teachers, Lord
and we pray that You will watch over them always--
these special people who hold our children
and our future in their hands.
Amen.

By Joanna Fuchs

Now That You're Retiring

Now that you're retiring
We can tell you how we feel;
Our heartfelt admiration
Is deeply felt and real.

You've been a great role model
For teachers and each kid;
You showed us how to be
In everything you did.

We'll miss your fine example;
We'll miss the things you gave;
Our pleasant memories of you
We'll recall and carefully save.

We wish for your retirement
The best of all your days;
May you discover sweet fulfillment
In new and rewarding ways.

By Joanna Fuchs

As You Retire

As you retire,
know that we will miss you.
Every day, we will feel a gap,
an empty space in our lives
that used to be filled
with the pleasure of seeing you.
As you retire,
look back on your major accomplishment:
the lives you touched, influenced,
and improved forever.
As you retire,
know how important you are to everyone,
a gem, a unique treasure
that we could never replace.
As you retire,
be fulfilled, be happy, be at peace;
you deserve it.

By Joanna Fuchs

THANKSGIVING POEMS

General Thanksgiving Poems

Thanksgiving Feasting

When the Halloween pumpkins are gone,
And the leaves have all fallen to ground,
When the air has turned windy and cold,
Then Thanksgiving will soon be around.

Thoughts of loved ones all feasting together,
Pleasant pictures from past times appear,
To dwell in each heart and each mind--
Then Thanksgiving is finally here!

The kitchen has scrumptious aromas,
The dining room looks oh, so fine,
Decorations with pilgrims and turkeys,
And now we are ready to dine!

First the napkins are placed on our laps;
Now the prayer for the meal to be blessed,
Then we stuff the good food in our tummies,
And we hope for it all to digest!

By Joanna Fuchs

Thank You For Inviting Us

Thank you for inviting us
To your Thanksgiving dinner.
A day spent in your company
Is invariably a winner.

Thank you for the time you spent
Preparing all the food;
For making us feel welcome,
You have our gratitude!

By Joanna Fuchs

More Than A Day

As Thanksgiving Day rolls around,
It brings up some facts, quite profound.
We may think that we're poor,
Feel like bums, insecure,
But in truth, our riches astound.

We have friends and family we love;
We have guidance from heaven above.
We have so much more
Than they sell in a store,
We're wealthy, when push comes to shove.

So add up your blessings, I say;
Make Thanksgiving last more than a day.
Enjoy what you've got;
Realize it's a lot,
And you'll make all your cares go away.

By Karl Fuchs

Thanksgiving Delights

On Thanksgiving Day we're thankful for
Our blessings all year through,
For family we dearly love,
For good friends, old and new.

For sun to light and warm our days,
For stars that glow at night,
For trees of green and skies of blue,
And puffy clouds of white.

We're grateful for our eyes that see
The beauty all around,
For arms to hug, and legs to walk,
And ears to hear each sound.

The list of all we're grateful for
Would fill a great big book;
Our thankful hearts find new delights
Everywhere we look!

By Joanna Fuchs

I'm Thankful for You

Thanksgiving is the appointed time
for focusing on the good in our lives.
In each of our days,
we can find small blessings,
but too often we overlook them,
choosing instead to spend our time
paying attention to problems.
We give our energy
to those who cause us trouble
instead of those who bring peace.
Starting now,
let's be on the lookout
for the bits of pleasure in each hour,
and appreciate the people who
bring love and light to everyone
who is blessed to know them.
You are one of those people.
On Thanksgiving,
I'm thankful for you.

By Joanna Fuchs

You've Made A Difference

As Thanksgiving Day approaches,
Our blessings we recall;
The things we are most thankful for,
We recollect them all.

You are really special,
In all you say and do.
You've made a difference in our lives;
We're thankful now for you.

By Joanna Fuchs

Thanksgiving Friends

Thanksgiving is a time
For reviewing what we treasure,
The people we hold dear,
Who give us so much pleasure.

Without you as my friend,
Life would be a bore;
Having you in my life
Is what I'm thankful for.

By Joanna Fuchs

Thanksgiving Every Day

The table is brimming with good things to eat;
We're surrounded by family and friends; what a treat.
The feelings that fill us today can't be beat;
It's Thanksgiving Day, and it all feels complete.

But other days, sometimes, things don't seem so fine;
Those days are not polished and don't seem to shine.
It's then in our minds, we forget all the good,
And think of the things we would get, if we could.

On days when our thinking causes us dread,
If we could remember, it's all in our head,
And not let our minds take our gratitude away,
Then we'd make every day like Thanksgiving Day.

By Karl Fuchs

A Family Thanksgiving

Mom and Dad And all the folks
who sit around the table,
all give thanks to the Lord above
for the fact that we are able
to have the food and shelter
we all need to survive,
and have the love of family
that makes it good to be alive.

By Karl Fuchs

A Child's Thanksgiving Thanks

I'm thankful for the many things
That help us live as well as kings,
For all the food that makes us drool,
And another holiday from school.

By Karl Fuchs

Thanksgiving Thoughts

Mom is in the kitchen,
And when I take a look,
I'm glad I'm not a turkey
That's she's about to cook!

By Karl Fuchs

Countdown To Thanksgiving

One two three,
A turkey in a tree;
Four five six,
That turkey's in a fix;
Seven eight nine,
It always tastes so fine;
When we get to ten
It's Thanksgiving once again.

By Karl Fuchs

Hooray For Thanksgiving

It's Thanksgiving dinner;
Let's not be late;
There's lots of good food,
So fill up your plate.
With pie at the end,

It can't be beat;
Hooray for Thanksgiving,
There's so much to eat!

By Karl Fuchs

Save Room

As meals go, Thanksgiving dinner
Is always a feast--a five star winner.
Here comes the salad, dressed just right,
The golden brown turkey--a savory delight;

The stuffing now, and then the gravy,
The Jell-O mold, all wiggly and wavy.
Take some cranberry sauce and candied yams;
Is there room for fresh made rolls and jams?

More dishes tempt me; ah, but I
Must save some room for pumpkin pie!

By Joanna Fuchs

Funny Thanksgiving Poems

Thanksgiving Ghost

The last piece of apple pie is gone;
How did it disappear?
The bowl of delicious stuffing
Has also vanished, I fear.

It happens each Thanksgiving,
When leftover goodies flee,
And each of us knows the responsible one
Couldn't be you or me.

The only way it could happen
Is readily diagnosed;
It must be the crafty, incredibly sneaky,
Still hungry Thanksgiving ghost.

By Karl Fuchs

Your Secret's Secure

Thanksgiving's the time in November each year
When our thoughts about food seem to richen,
When turkey and dressing and other good stuff
Is being prepared in the kitchen.

But the stores did their homework way in advance;
They know what your real needs will be;
They know you'll come shopping to buy up their best,
And those sharing your feast will soon see...

You're the best cook in town, a peerless gourmet,
The turkey, dessert and the wine;
And your secret's secure that this feast was all made
By your grocery, and they sure did it fine!

By Karl and Joanna Fuchs

Belly Stuffer

Thanksgiving brings a terrible chore,
'Cause I'm forced to eat and eat some more.
If I don't eat it up right down to dessert,
I fear the cook's feelings will be very hurt,
So I do my part, even though I suffer;
To be a good guest, I'm a belly stuffer.

By Karl Fuchs

Thanksgiving $$$

Why do we celebrate Thanksgiving Day?
What's its significance? all of us say.
We all find importance for which we are thankful,
And what we spend on this holiday is surely a bank full.

First the purchase of food for parties galore,
Then the fuel and decorating costs come to the fore.
We eat so much food that many get ill,
And drug makers get richer with each little pill.

It all becomes clear, if we closely examine
That we're not giving thanks for avoiding a famine;
We're creating the wealth and the plenty we see,
Including the sports ads we watch on TV.

By Karl Fuchs

Thanksgiving Prayers

Abundant Blessing

We thank you for the turkey,
The gravy and the dressing;
Dear Lord, this table overflows
With Thy abundant blessing.

Let us always be aware
That all gifts come from You,
And may we serve Your heavenly will
In everything we do.

By Joanna Fuchs

Thankful for Each Other

Dear Lord,
As we gather together around this table
laden with your plentiful gifts to us,
we thank You for always providing
what we really need
and for sometimes granting wishes
for things we don't really need.
Today, let us be especially thankful
for each other--for family and friends
who enrich our lives in wonderful ways,
even when they present us with challenges.
Let us join together now
in peaceful, loving fellowship
to celebrate Your love for us
and our love for each other. Amen.

By Joanna Fuchs

Thanksgiving Blessings

Lord, as we bow our heads to pray,
We celebrate Thanksgiving Day.
Help us have the right attitude,
As we turn to you in gratitude.

Thank you for our festive mood;
Thank you, Lord, for this good food;
Thanks for blessings great and small;
Thank you, thank you for it all.

By Joanna Fuchs

For All that You Give Us

Dear Lord,
On this Thanksgiving Day,
we are thankful
for all that You give us,
all that You do for us,
all that You teach us.
Thank You for guiding us
to live our lives
in Your will,
Your purpose,
Your plan for us.
Thank You for Your protection
from worldly influence and danger.
Thank You for bringing us gently
to a deeper knowledge of You
and what You want from us,
with Your love, mercy,
compassion and grace.
And thank you, Lord,
for the blessings
we are experiencing right now
at this very moment--
the food,
and the precious people who are with us
to enjoy this meal and this day.
Thank You, Lord. Amen.

By Joanna Fuchs

Attitude of Gratitude

Dear Lord, we come to You today
With a humble attitude.
For all you give, our hearts are full
Of love and gratitude.

Thank you for this special time
To offer our Thanksgiving.
Thank you for this food, and for
The blessed lives we're living.

By Joanna Fuchs

We Are Thankful

Dear Lord,
we are thankful for this day,
set aside to honor all the ways You bless us
with Your goodness, love, and grace.
We are thankful for the people at this table
who add a variety of wonderful things to our lives
just by being who they are.
We are thankful for the food we are about to eat,
which You created for our nourishment and pleasure.
Most of all, Lord, we thank You
for always being there for us,
guiding us, encouraging us,
comforting us and blessing us.
In Jesus' name we pray; Amen.

By Joanna Fuchs

Another Good Year

We thank you, Lord, for food and friends
And for all of the joy this holiday lends;
It's Thanksgiving Day and we can see
The blessings you've provided our family.

Thanks to you, Lord, for another good year;
When you watch over us, there's nothing to fear.

By Karl Fuchs

Two-Line Thanksgiving Prayers for Kids

Lord, we thank you this Thanksgiving,
For the food we eat and the lives we're living. Amen.

Lord, we pray You'll bless this food,
As we eat it now in gratitude. Amen.

We thank You, God, for the food we eat;
We thank you for our lives so sweet. Amen.

By Joanna Fuchs

Thanksgiving Dinner Poem, Song and Prayer

(To the tune of "We Gather Together")

Our table is set now; great food you can bet now.
It's Thanksgiving Day, and we're ready to eat;
All those near and dear us are here today to cheer us.
This dinner is a winner, a wonderful treat.

It's time to be thankful for all that God gives us;
Dear Lord, we are grateful; Dear God, hear our prayer.
It's You we are praising; our voices we are raising;
Bless us and bless this food; keep us safe in your care.

By Joanna Fuchs

THANK YOU POEMS

General Thank You Poems

Thank You!

I really appreciate you,
Your helpful, giving ways,
And how your generous heart
Your unselfishness displays.

I thank you for your kindness,
I will not soon forget;
You're one of the nicest people
I have ever met.

By Joanna Fuchs

You Didn't Have To

Thank you for what you did;
You didn't have to do it.
I'm glad someone like you
Could help me to get through it.

I'll always think of you
With a glad and grateful heart;
You are very special;
I knew it from the start!

By Joanna Fuchs

Help and Caring

Thanks for doing what you did;
You are kind beyond belief;
Your help and caring calmed me down,
And gave me soothing relief.

By Karl and Joanna Fuchs

It Doesn't Seem Enough

I want to tell you "Thank you,"
But it doesn't seem enough.
Words don't seem sufficient--
"Blah, blah" and all that stuff.

Please know I have deep feelings
About your generous act.
I really appreciate you;
You're special, and that's a fact!

By Joanna Fuchs

Thank You for Being You

Thank you for (the gift/your kindness).
Thank you for being the person you are:
kind and thoughtful,
sensitive and considerate,
a generous and thoughtful giver.
You are unselfish always,
putting others before yourself,
making me/us feel special and important.
It is a privilege and a pleasure to know you.

By Joanna Fuchs

For All You Do

Thank you so much for all you do;
You're truly a delight;
When my life overwhelms and does me in,
You make everything all right.

By Karl and Joanna Fuchs

I Appreciate You

You are a person
who makes life easier and better
for everyone around you.
Your continual acts

of thoughtfulness and kindness
brighten each day.
What you did for me
will glow in my memory,
reviving pleasant feelings
every time I think about it.
I appreciate you, and I thank you.

By Joanna Fuchs

Your Loving Heart

You touch my life with your kindness;
You know just what I need.
Your loving heart shows its caring
In your every thought and deed.

By Joanna Fuchs

You Made My Day

I appreciate your kindness
More than words can say;
The very nice thing you did for me
Really made my day!

By Joanna Fuchs

You Care About People

You care about people
and it shows.
You are generous with your time,
giving of your energy,
lavish with your unselfish deeds.
I will remember your kindness to me.
Thank you for brightening my world
with your thoughtfulness.
It really meant a lot.

By Joanna Fuchs

Thanks for the Good Times

Thank you for the good times,
The days you filled with pleasure.
Thank you for fond memories,
And for feelings I'll always treasure.

By Karl Fuchs

Thank You for the Gift Poems

Lovely Gift

Wow, thank you for the lovely gift;
It's something I would choose.
It gave my spirits quite a lift,
It's something I will use!

By Karl Fuchs

Special Gift

This is just to let you know
How special your gift made me feel.
It shows me how very thoughtful you are;
Your gift to me was ideal!

By Karl Fuchs

Thoughtful gift

Thank you for the lovely gift;
You didn't have to do it.
You have a good and gracious heart,
But then, I always knew it.

I love this, and I think of you
With fondness and with pleasure;
The gift is great, but even more,
It's your thoughtfulness I treasure.

By Joanna Fuchs

You're Our Rock

Thank you, caring pastor
For tending to your flock;
You keep us all from weakening;
Like Jesus, you're our rock.

Thank you special pastor;
Your sheep you're always feeding;
Through example, guidance and stirring talks,
You give us what we're needing.

Thank you, Pastor, for teaching
About Jesus, our Lord and Master;
For all you say and are and do,
Thank you, thank you, pastor!

By Joanna Fuchs

VALENTINE POEMS

Compatible Valentine

On Valentine's Day, we think about
The people who are dear,
How much they add to life's delight
Whenever they are near.

You've always been a total joy,
Such pleasant company,
I very much appreciate
Our compatibility!

By Joanna Fuchs

Essential Valentine

On Valentine's Day we think about
Those matchless people who
Give extra meaning to our lives--
The very special few.

Without them, skies would turn to gray;
Things wouldn't be the same;
Life wouldn't be as colorful;
It would be a duller game.

And when I contemplate that group--
Friends and family who are mine,
I appreciate and treasure you;
You're essential, Valentine!

By Joanna Fuchs

198

Valentine Treasures

Valentine treasures are people who
have often crossed your mind,
family, friends and others, too,
who in your life have shined
the warmth of love or a spark of light
that makes you remember them;
no matter how long since you've actually met,
each one is a luminous gem,
who gleams and glows in your memory,
bringing special pleasures,
and that's why this Valentine comes to you:
You're one of those sparkling treasures!

By Joanna Fuchs

Wherever I May Go

You're in my thoughts and in my heart
Wherever I may go;
On Valentine's Day, I'd like to say
I care more than you know.

By Joanna Fuchs

Special People

On Valentine's Day, we think of people
who have cheered and encouraged us,
who go out of their way
to be kind and caring,
who have enriched our lives
just by being themselves.
You are such a person.
I'm so happy you're my _____
(friend, aunt, co-worker, etc.)
Happy Valentine's Day!

By Joanna Fuchs

Special Connection

Valentine's Day is for expressing affection;
Fond thoughts are coming your way;
We've always had a special connection,
So Happy Valentine's Day!

By Joanna Fuchs

Pleasant Thoughts of You

Whenever likable people cross my mind,
I always have such pleasant thoughts of you.
You bring me so much happiness and joy;
Those who lift me up are very few.

On Valentine's Day I want to tell you this:
Knowing you is an extraordinary pleasure;
Your caring heart is always quick to give;
You're unique, a rare and very special treasure.

By Joanna Fuchs

Valentine Gift

On Valentine's Day,
I'm thinking about the special ways
you have made my life better;
the little things, the not-so-little things...
your kindness, the way you always listen
and pay attention to me.
You make my world brighter and richer.
You're a gift to me,
and I thank you for being you.

By Joanna Fuchs

Valentine Smile

On Valentine's Day we think of those
Who make our lives worthwhile,
Those gracious, friendly people who
We think of with a smile.

I am fortunate to know you,
That's why I want to say,
To a rare and special person:
Happy Valentine's Day!

By Joanna Fuchs

Roses Are Red...

Roses are red; daisies are white;
Valentine, you make every day a delight.
Violets are blue; daffodils are yellow;
Valentine, you make my heart jiggle like Jell-O!

By Joanna Fuchs

Terrific Person

Hey you—you're often on my mind;
You're a terrific person, one of a kind.
I'm sending this poem, because I want to say
I'm thinking of you on Valentine's Day!

By Joanna Fuchs

Top of the List

On Valentine's Day,
when I think of the people
I care about and value,
you are at the top of the list.
Like a rainbow
glistening through the rain,
like a glowing green spring
after a cold gray winter,
you are a joy and a delight.
Like a good book, a cozy fire,
or a cup of cocoa (with marshmallows),
you are a comfort to me.
I appreciate you.
Happy Valentine's Day!

By Joanna Fuchs

Special Valentine

Special people are on my mind
Each year on Valentine's Day,
The exceptional ones who mean to me
More than I can say.

I respect you and admire you,
And I just want you to know
You've made a difference in my life
And I want to tell you so.

By Joanna Fuchs

Glad to Know You

On Valentine's Day, the day of affection,
Our thoughts quickly turn in your direction.
This Valentine poem is meant to show you
How very glad we are to know you!

By Joanna Fuchs

Valentine Gem

Valentine, you are a gem;
You fill my life with joy and pleasure;
With all you give and all you do,
You're a very special treasure.

I really like the person you are;
You're a class act, in every way;
I care about you, and I hope you have
A very happy Valentine's Day!

By Joanna Fuchs

A Valentine for my Teacher

Every day I come to school;
I spend a lot of time
Learning all the things you teach,
Which is the reason I'm
Sending you this Valentine;
It's meant to let you know
I'm happy you're my teacher
And I want to tell you so!

By Joanna Fuchs

Christian Valentine Poems

I Corinthians 13

Valentine's Day is a day of love,
For showing that we care,
And if we read the Bible,
God describes love there:

If we speak like celestial angels
From heaven up above,
All our words mean nothing
If we don't have Christian love.

Love is patient, love is kind;
It doesn't brag or boast;
Love conquers pride and envy;
It is never self-engrossed.

Love is not rude or angry;
Forgiveness counters wrong;
Love stays away from evil;
It sings a truthful song.

Love is full of trust and hope;
It always perseveres;
Love never fails; It's faithful;
To the Bible it adheres.

And if you give this kind of love
To your special Valentine,
You'll be loving right in harmony
With God's own sweet design.

By Joanna Fuchs

God's Valentine Gift

God's Valentine gift of love to us
Was not a bunch of flowers;
It wasn't candy, or a book
To while away the hours.

His gift was to become a man,
So He could freely give
His sacrificial love for us,
So you and I could live.

He gave us sweet salvation, and
Instruction, good and true--
To love our friends and enemies
And love our Savior, too.

So as we give our Valentines,
Let's thank our Lord and King;
The reason we have love to give
Is that He gave everything.

By Joanna Fuchs

You Are Often In My Thoughts

Love is a command
That Christians are called to do;
Our Lord says "Love your God,
And love your neighbor, too."

Some people are easy to love;
They are human rays of sun;
They light up every life,
And encourage everyone.

You are in that group,
So I sincerely want to say:
You are often in my thoughts;
Happy Valentine's Day!

By Joanna Fuchs

What Valentine Can I Give Him?

What can I give to Jesus
On this special Valentine's Day?
How can I tell Him I'll love Him,
And follow Him, come what may?

How can I show I need Him?
Should I send a red heart, with lace?
How can I thank Him enough
For his sacrifice, love and grace?

What Valentine can I give Him,
My adoration to impart?
I'll give to Him what He wants most;
I'll yield to Him my heart.

By Joanna Fuchs

Twice As Sweet

On Valentines Day, we show our love;
We express our deep affections.
Those who are important to us
Get cards and sweet confections.

But Christian love is not just for
The ones we hold most dear;
Jesus said "love everyone;"
He made that very clear.

For Christians, it is every day
We should care and love and serve
Everyone we meet in life,
Whether they do or don't deserve.

Let's follow Jesus' good command
To love everyone we meet.
Valentine's Day every day
Will make life twice as sweet.

By Joanna Fuchs

Valentine's Day Is for Christian Love

Valentine's Day is for honoring love;
To show those we love we care.
Red hearts with tender sentiments
We send, our love to share.

So on Valentine's Day we're reminded
Of our very first Christian goal:
To love the Lord with all our heart
And all our mind and soul.

To love our neighbor as ourselves
We are also told to do,
So let's live our love by the Bible;
It's God's word, flawless and true.

If we give this Christian Valentine first,
We'll never run out of love,
For infinite love will come to us
From God in heaven above.

By Joanna Fuchs

Valentine Divine

When Jesus Christ decided to
Give us a Valentine,
He followed His Father's orders--
The task God did assign.

He gave Himself, His life, His all,
For this special Valentine,
Knowing He would change the world;
Real love He'd redefine.

It's sacrifice we need to give
To a beloved Valentine;
When we do that, we get a glimpse
Of the holy and divine.

Oh Lord, please help us be like you,
With every Valentine.
When we love each other as You did,
It's then that we're really Thine.

By Joanna Fuchs

Christian Valentine Love Poem

On Valentine's Day
I reaffirm my deep and abiding love for you.
I continually pray to love you
like Jesus loves:
wholly, selflessly, completely.
I continually pray
to be the person
God wants me to be for you.
I appreciate you
for your heart full of love for me,
your dependably fine character
and for the special gifts God has given you,
that I notice and admire and treasure.
I am abundantly blessed
that you are mine eternally.
Happy Valentine's Day, Sweetheart;
My heart and my love are yours forever.

By Joanna Fuchs

Family Valentine Poems

Your Family Is Like That

Sometimes a group of people
Will bring you happiness
In ways you never dreamed of,
In ways you can't express.

Your family is like that;
That's why we want to say
How much we appreciate you;
Happy Valentine's Day!

By Joanna Fuchs

A Valentine Poem for My ____

On Valentine's Day, the day of affection,
My thoughts naturally turn in your direction.
I think of many things, big and small
That you've given to me and given your all.
You see me always in the kindest light;
You're a glow in my life, golden and bright.
I'm thankful for the happy ties that bind
Me to you in our family, and I'd like to remind
You of all the special memories I treasure;
Having you in my life is nothing but pleasure!
You're a walking example of how to live,
How to share, how to teach, how to love, how to give.

Please accept this Valentine poem,
warm from the heart of your _____

By Joanna Fuchs

Daughter Valentine Poems

Wonderful Daughter

You're a wonderful daughter;
You fill me with lots of pride.
Do you have more smarts than beauty?
I can never decide.

You're a very special person,
So on this Valentines Day,
I want you to know you're loved
Forever, not just today.

By Karl Fuchs

Valentine Daughter

You're my wonderful daughter,
The absolute gem of my life.
Always a joy and a pleasure,
Through good times and through strife.

I love how you chip in,
Whenever there's work to be done.
I love your contagious laugh,
When you're just having fun.

I love everything about you,
And is why I say,
Be my Valentine daughter,
Every Valentines Day!

By Karl and Joanna Fuchs

Valentine Doll

Of all the games I used to play
When I came home from school each day,
Playing a mother was my favorite one;
I'd play with my dolls and have lots of fun.

Now I'm a real mom, and I still love to play
With my real live doll named_____ each day.
I love my Valentine dolly who's living
And walking and talking, and loving and giving.

So daughter, as I watch you grow,
I'll love you more, and I want you to know,
My heart is yours, honey, come what may,
Every day of the year, not just Valentine's Day.

By Joanna Fuchs

My Daughter

My wonderful daughter, delight of my heart,
I hope that you know you're both lovely and smart.
I cherish you dearly for the person you are,
You have passion and caring that will carry you far.

Wherever you go you'll be watched by my love,
And we'll always be close, like a hand in a glove.
May the years treat you kindly, may laughter hold sway,
And I'm here for you always if your blue skies turn gray.

By Karl Fuchs

Son Valentine Poems

Treasured Son

On Valentine's Day, parents think
About the ones they treasure,
And you, son, are a special joy;
You bring us so much pleasure.

We hoped for much and got much more;
We're oh so proud of you.
Sons so special and so loved
Are very, very few.

By Joanna Fuchs

Happy Valentine's Day, Son

Happy Valentine's Day to our wonderful son,
We love you a lot, you should know.
On this special day, we remind you again;
We love you wherever you go.

Strange as this might seem to you now,
When you're a dad and have kids of your own,
You'll then understand the love that we feel
For you, and the way that you've grown.

By Karl Fuchs

My Son

My son, you're a remarkable person to me;
Your good qualities make me feel proud.
I don't give you compliments often enough,
But I really should shout them out loud.

You're an intelligent, capable, likeable guy;
I often admire what you do.
You've got a good heart; you help and you care;
To your family and friends you are true.

You're responsible, trustworthy, faithful and kind;
You work hard to do all you can.
My heart fills with joy when I think to myself
That I raised such a wonderful man.

By Joanna and Karl Fuchs

Sister Valentine Poems

Sisters Heart to Heart

From the time that we were little,
I knew you'd always be
Not just a loving sister
But a caring friend to me.

A shoulder I could cry on,
A helping hand in times of need,
A cheerleader to lift me up,
My angel in both word and deed.

We told each other secrets;
We giggled and we cried.
We shared our joys and sorrows--
We were always side by side.

We have a very special bond;
I knew it from the start.
You'll have my love forever--
We're sisters, heart to heart.

By Joanna Fuchs

Glad You're Mine

A message to my (Name):
Hey, be my Valentine!
I'm happy to have a sister,
And I'm really glad you're mine!

All the fun we shared,
Being friends and siblings, too
Makes me really grateful
To have a sister just like you!

By Joanna Fuchs

Brother Valentine Poem

Special Brother

(Name), I think of you a lot;
You're my very special brother;
Even if I could choose anyone,
I'd never settle for any other.

You're really smart and kind and strong;
I'm glad that you are mine;
To show how very much I care,
I'm sending this Valentine!

By Joanna Fuchs

Mother Valentine Poems

Forever Valentine Mom

Valentine's Day is a day of love,
So Mom, I want to say
That no one gives more love than you;
You brighten every day.

You deserve my undying love;
You earned it from the start,
So on Valentine's Day I give to you
A forever place in my heart.

By Joanna Fuchs

Mother Valentine's Day Poem

Mom, on Valentine's Day I am reminded
that no one in my life
gives more love than you do.
You care so deeply and give so much;
Without you,
I couldn't be the person I am.
You are the foundation of my life.
Your encouragement and support
make everything seem possible,
because I know
you'll always be there for me,
to cheer me, to comfort me,
to give me a boost when I need it.
On Valentine's Day I want you to know
that I love you, I appreciate you,
and I feel so blessed that you are my mother!

By Joanna Fuchs

Dear Mother of Mine

Dear mother of mine, you're the best; there's no doubt,
So on Valentine's Day to the world I will shout:

"My mother is kind and she's smart as a whip,
And she guides me in life as you'd steer a big ship.
She helps me to see the good from the bad;
I bet she's the best Mom that ever was had."

You're one great mom, I'm happy to say,
And I love you a lot on this Valentine's Day!

By Karl Fuchs

Father Valentine Poem

Valentine Dad

I'm thinking of you on Valentine's Day;
I love and admire you, Dad.
I'll always remember and cherish a lot
The good times that we had.

You were the very first man in my life,
You showed me how good men should be.
I'm grateful that you're my father, Dad,
So Happy Valentine's Day, from me.

By Joanna Fuchs

Parents Valentine Poem

Valentine Poem For Parents

Mom and Dad, along life's path,
Your love has shone the way.
For the guidance you have given me,
I'm thankful every day.

You've always been great parents;
I'm so glad you both are mine;
Deep in my heart, you'll always be
My favorite Valentine.

By Joanna Fuchs

Grandparents Valentine Poems

Valentine's Day Poem For Grandma

Dear Grandma, you have always been to me
A giver of sweet, unconditional love,
A soft and gentle presence in my life,
My angel, who was sent from heaven above.

I want to tell you now, on Valentine's Day,
I love you, and I think you're really great;
You're everything a grandmother should be;
A cherished person I appreciate!

By Joanna Fuchs

A Gift I Can't Repay

Grandma and Grandpa, you're my Valentine;
You make a difference in my life each day;
Because I have your unconditional love,
You've given me a gift I can't repay.

If I could make the world a better place,
If there were just one thing that I could do,
To make each person happy and at peace,
I'd give them all grandparents just like you!

By Joanna Fuchs

Grandparents Meet A Need

Grandparents meet a need
That no one else can fill;
They're always kind and gentle;
They love you and always will.

They have plenty of time to listen,
To encourage and to care;
When others are too busy,
Grandparents are always there.

They have delicious foods;
There's always something cooking;
They feed you scrumptious tidbits,
When no one else is looking.

They take you special places;
They're never in a hurry.
They soothe you when you're troubled,
And help you not to worry.

They buy you things you want,
Even things that you don't need;
"Do what makes them happy!"
Is every grandparent's creed.

They focus on your good points,
And overlook each flaw;
How could we do without
Our grandma and grandpa?

Thank you, Grandpa and Grandma,
For giving life a special shine;
I'm glad to have grandparents,
And happy you both are mine!

By Joanna Fuchs

Wife Valentine Poems

I'm Thankful That I Married You

I'm thankful that I married you;
You're always there for me, on my side;
You're a wonderful woman, my cherished wife;
When you're with me, I'm filled with special pride.

You always look for ways to help;
I'm so very grateful for all you do.
You make my life much happier,
With little things, and big things, too.

I love you, and I always will;
I'm so very glad that you are mine.
You're all I'll ever need or want;
My precious wife, my Valentine.

By Joanna Fuchs

For My Precious Wife

This Valentine is for you, my precious wife,
Because you're the adorable love of my life.
Your many fine qualities deserve praise to the skies,
For you are sweet, kind, caring and wise.

It's hard to recount all the good times with you;
There are so many wonderful things that you do,
That the pleasures just mingle, and tingle my soul,
So that loving you better is always my goal.

It's hard to imagine a more perfect life
Than the one I am living with you as my wife.
All the good things I could ever desire,
I find in you, partner; you light my fire!

By Karl Fuchs

My Pride and My Pleasure

My dear partner and wife,
You're the love of my life,
And I love you much more every year.

You are kind, and you're sweet,
And your thinking's so neat,
That I always learn lots from you, dear.

You are generous and charming,
With a smile that's disarming;
You are truly my pride and my pleasure.

All the things that are you
Make my dreams all come true,
And for always your love I will treasure!

By Karl Fuchs

Special Wife

Dear one, you're my sweetheart,
My companion and my wife;
Please be my Valentine;
Be my partner all through life.

The years will bring life's beauty,
As my love for you still grows,
Like the rose bush blooms in springtime,
To produce the perfect rose.

When I was young I dreamed
That life could be such fun,
Filled with joy and adventure,
If I could find the one.

Now you're at my side;
At last my dream is true,
I'm a very lucky man
To have a special wife like you!

By Karl Fuchs

Perfect Valentine Wife

Each day you fill my heart with love;
My wife, you're a blessing from up above.
I have a partner whose life I share,
A sweetheart who's beyond compare.

You're a wondrous delight, my Valentine,
And I'm very thankful you are mine.
You're cute and smart and caring, too;
It was my lucky day when I found you.

You're the perfect blend of wife for me;
In my eyes you shine, so I hope you see
How my love for you grows; it's deep and strong,
As we share our days in our own love song.

By Karl Fuchs

Husband Valentine Poems

Ideal Valentine Husband

How can I tell you how much I care,
This year on Valentine's Day?
Words can't express the depth of my love,
No matter what I say.

Should I say you're an ideal husband?
That's absolutely true.
Or should I fall back on the old standby,
And simply say "I love you?"

No, that won't do for such a special man,
Not that ordinary stuff.
Nothing I say about how much I feel,
Will ever be enough.

By Joanna Fuchs

Husband Valentine Poem

Happy Valentines Day to my husband;
You're still the one for me.
Though the years go by, I love you still,
As all the world can see.

You were quite a guy when you caught my eye,
Those many years ago.
Though you're older now, you're still "the man."
I just thought you'd want to know.

By Karl Fuchs

Friend Valentine Poems

Complete Valentine Friend

A friend is like a Valentine
She has a loving heart.
You share with her your feelings;

Her listening is an art.

A friend is like a Valentine;
Like candy, she is sweet.
And that description fits you, friend;
You make my life complete!

By Joanna Fuchs

Cherished Valentine Friend

Valentine's Day is all about
Special feelings warm and fond,
And friend, I knew right from the start
We had a very special bond.

Our time together is a gift;
You're interesting and warm and fun!
And when I need to talk and share,
I think of you, friend; you're the one.

We're always true and real together.
We have no reason to pretend.
I'm thankful that you're in my life,
My trusted, cherished Valentine friend.

By Joanna Fuchs

A Friend Is Like A Valentine

A friend is like a Valentine
Heartwarming, bringing pleasure.
Connected to good feelings,
With memories to treasure.

Seeing a special Valentine
Brings happiness to stay;
And that's what you do, friend.
You brighten every day!

By Joanna Fuchs

My Valentine Friend

Valentine's Day reminds me
how meaningful my feelings are for you.
You have a special place in my world
that no one else could fill.
Out of your overflowing heart,
you add color and light to my life.
You continually cross my mind,
like a precious dose of sunshine,
lighting me up inside as I think of you
and the lasting memories
we have created together.
No Valentine gift is as precious to me
as you are,
my Valentine friend.

By Joanna Fuchs

My Shining Friend

People come and people go,
In and out of your life and so,
When one shines bright among the rest,
And is there when needed, you're truly blessed.
That is how I see you, friend of mine,
And why I'm sending this Valentine.

By Karl Fuchs

Our Lives Entwine

You'll never know what you mean to me,
And how important you've come to be.
We share special days as our lives entwine,
And that's why I send you this Valentine.

By Karl Fuchs

Valentine Friend

A Valentine friend is someone you choose
To share your life with you,
Someone who is always there,
Whether you're happy or blue.

With a Valentine friend, you can be yourself
You don't need to pretend;
When you're careful to choose a compatible match,
You create a perfect blend.

With you for my special Valentine friend,
My life is full and bright;
You bring contentment, joy and peace;
You're my Valentine delight!

By Joanna Fuchs

Top of the List Valentine Friend

Thoughts of affection fill my mind
When Valentine's Day is near;
I think about my closest friends,
Those who are most dear.

And on that special Valentine list,
You're at the top, my friend.
I love you, and I know for sure,
Our friendship will never end!

By Joanna Fuchs

Perfect Valentine Friend

If I could create the perfect friend,
One of my own design,
A friend to be my companion,
A friend for a Valentine,

I'd build her with a giving heart
Filled with kindness, too,
A friend who's also lots of fun,
But I've already got one--you!

By Joanna Fuchs

What Can I Say?

What can I say to let you know
that your friendship means everything to me.
How can I make you aware
that my life is so much better and happier
because you're in it.
What can I do to convey how I feel—
that I'm blessed in so many ways
to have you as my friend.
Will this little rhyme help?

You've always been a friend so fine;
Will you be my Valentine?

By Joanna Fuchs

Friendship Valentine Poem

Friendship is a wondrous thing;
There's so much happiness it can bring.
I'm really glad that you're my friend,
And I hope our friendship will never end.

By Karl Fuchs

Best Friend Valentine

On Valentine's Day, the day of affection,
I'm sending fond thoughts in your direction.
You're really special, my perfect friend;
Together, we are a perfect blend.

You give my life a special shine;
Will you be my best friend Valentine?

By Joanna Fuchs

Since My Valentine Got A Computer

Since my Valentine got a computer
My love life has taken a hit.
Nothing I say is important
Unless it's a byte or a bit.

Before she got her new laptop,
Everything was just fine;
Now she says we can't talk
Unless we both go online.

"But honey," I said, "I'm attached to you;
Love is what I feel."
"That keyword isn't relevant,"
She said, with eyes of steel.

She clicked the keyboard furiously;
The screen was all she could see,
And then to my horror and shame,
She started describing me:

"Your motherboard needs upgrading;
Your OS needs help, too.
And you definitely need a big heat sink
To cool your CPU."

"Don't flame me, my sweet," I pleaded.
"Not on Valentine's Day."
"Fix the bugs, and I'll see," she said,
While looking at me with dismay.

"What ever you want, my darling;
Whatever you need; you call it.
I'll upload or download anything,
And then I'll go install it."

(Her hostile CD keeps replaying,
And though I don't want to fight her,
Is this what I want for a Valentine?
I've been burned; can I rewrite her?)

"Are you all hard drive now," I asked
"Is there no software in you?
Don't you remember the good times?
Let our memories see us through."

"LOL," she said to me, chuckling.
"You're nothing but ad ware.
"I've got four gigs of memory;
I've got no problem there."

"Please, honey, we can save it," I said.
"Our love means more than that."
"That's not in my cache; we're going to crash,"
She said, as she turned me down flat.

(This woman has really changed;
Do I really want to chase her?
More and more I'm thinking
It might be nice to erase her.)

"Aw, honey, don't talk like that," I said.
"Can't we just plug and play?
I hereby accept default,
And I'm yours, my love, come what may.

My goal is to make you happy;
I want to be your portal,
But your sudden, distant coldness
Would test the strongest mortal.

If we need a brand new interface,
So we can FTP,
I'm your go along, get along guy,
And I want you to stay with me."

"If you want to get into my favorites," she said,
And you want to get past my encryption,
If you want to get through my firewall,
Here is my only prescription."

"First, put up your own Web site,
And e-mail me when it's done.
I'll check your page rank with Google,
And tell you if you're the one."

My life has become a real trial,
Since my Valentine got a computer.
If I want her to care about me again,
I guess I'll have to reboot her.

By Joanna Fuchs

Valentine Zoo

I'm an animal lover, I'm happy to say.
And I love them and pet them most every day.
So for you, Valentine, I thank heaven above,
Because you're so much like the creatures I love.

You're cuddly and cute as a warm, playful kitten,
With your animal nature, my love, I am smitten.
You walk like a lioness stalking the plain,
With your dangerous eyes and your beautiful mane.

It's such pleasure to pet you, as you sigh and you purr,
I run my hand over you, like stroking your fur.
I'm the strong Alpha wolf, with you at my side,
Sharing love, food and shelter, and feelings of pride.

These feelings of animal love we can share,
As I find different ways to show that I care.
So won't you please be my own private zoo?
My Valentine, I love to play with you.

By Karl Fuchs

The Magic Valentine Potion

I was strong and now I'm weak,
So a secret potion now I seek,
To help me balance out my life,
To help me shed this inner strife.

What torment makes me whimper deep,
That keeps me nights without much sleep,
That took the strength from muscles strong,
That makes me hear the birdie's song.

This potion must be magic sweet,
To make me whole, again complete.
So be my potion, Valentine,
Just answer me that you'll be mine.

By Karl Fuchs

Valentine, You're Food For My Soul

From the moment we talked, I started to get
Feelings of hunger that couldn't be met,
Like feelings that come when I see yummy pies,
Well, I get those feelings when I look in your eyes.

The thought of your lips makes my mouth start to water,
'Cause they remind me of barbecue more than they oughter.
Your skin, your hair, and the rest of you brings
Thoughts of chocolate chip cookies and other good things.

When you're near you provide scrumptious food for my soul.
You nourish me, sweetheart; you make me whole.
Keep me satisfied, stay close or I'll pine.
I sure get hungry thinking of you, Valentine!

By Karl Fuchs

Hindsight

I said to you, "Oh, please be mine;
Be mine forever, Valentine."
I must have seemed like quite a fool,
Although I thought I was being cool.

I swore that we would never part,
As I put my hand upon my heart.
Had I been thinking with my head,
I'd probably have fled instead.

By Joanna Fuchs

Everything Reminds Me Of You

I look at a tree,
And what do I see?
My Valentine's face
Smiling back at me.

I spot a cute rock,
But, oh what a shock,
For it reminds of you
And that is no crock.

Everywhere that I turn,
My feelings just burn
With thoughts about you,
My love please don't spurn!

Each rock and each tree,
Each cloud and each bee,
The earth and the sea,
It all reminds me...

I love you awesomely!

By Karl Fuchs

Timeless Valentine

As time goes by from year to year,
One thing is surely true, my dear;
Though decades come and decades go,
Just seeing you sets me aglow.

Time shifts my body; I start to sag,
When I pass a mirror, it can make me gag.
My joints all ache; I can hardly move;
Still a smile from you, and I'm in the groove.

Getting older can be a pain,
But with you along, I can't complain.
Despite the things that we go through,
I know I'll never stop loving you.

Your loving heart turns life to play,
As we laugh at time from day to day.
So I write this poem, and I'll hang my sign,
Saying, "Always Be My Valentine."

By Karl and Joanna Fuchs

Superhero Valentine

Valentine, you're in my dreams,
Both daytime and at night;
I dream of how you'd feel to touch,
How I'd fill you with delight.

So far my dreams have not come true;
You scarcely know I'm there.
But if I were a super hero,
Then I could make you care.

As Spiderman I'd weave a web,
Lure you and catch you in it,
So you couldn't just smile and walk away,
After talking less than a minute.

As Plastic Man my parts could stretch,
I'd form them as you desire.
We could play till we got it right;
Now that should light your fire.

As Batman I'd show you sweet mysteries
In my secret underground lair.
I'd kiss and caress you to ecstasy;
Say yes; just take my dare.

I might be the superhero you've dreamed;
Don't automatically deny me.
Just put yourself in my loving hands;
You won't be sorry; try me.

You're my personal Wonder Woman;
Be my heroine, Valentine.
Let me show you why you should choose me,
And why you'll love being mine.

By Karl and Joanna Fuchs

Will You Be Mine?

Valentine, you make me silly;
You make my heart beat willy-nilly;
When I'm with you, the world is hazy;
Valentine, you drive me crazy!

Valentine, when we're apart,
My need for you goes off the chart.
Will you be mine? Can I be thine?
Say you'll be my Valentine!

By Joanna Fuchs

My Princess

Life was always quite normal and sane;
Now we've met and it's weakened my brain.

My whole life now is like a story book,
With a beautiful princess and villains that look
Like other men, but they're evil and bad;
They keep trying to make my princess so sad
By keeping her from me; it's driving me crazy,
But "happily ever after" is not for the lazy.

So I'll plan and I'll strive till my princess can see
That her handsome, courageous, hero is me.

That's what I dream;
To make my dreaming come true
The only thing needed is the presence of you
To be by my side, in the picture I see
As the princess I'll love for eternity.

By Karl Fuchs

Will You Be My Valentine?

For months I've sat and held it in,
It choked inside and hurt like sin.
It made me sweat and steam and stew,
Whenever I caught sight of you.

Thank goodness Valentine's Day has come;
If I held it longer, it would strike me dumb.
This day I'll say it, come rain or shine...
Will you be my Valentine?

By Karl Fuchs

I'd Like to Get to Know You

At first you were just a gleam in my eye,
Just a squiggly feeling when you would walk by.
Because you look like such a treat,
You've made mush of my brain, made me weak in the feet.

This can't go on, I've got to find out
What you are like, or without a doubt
My breathing will cease and my heart will go bust,
And all of my mechanisms will wither to dust.

I know what I'll do, I'll approach you and smile--
Say, "I'm lost" or "It's a great day" or something, or I'll
Pass out from fright and die of remorse.
Anyway, that won't really happen, of course.

I'll get up the nerve and say out of the blue...
"Hi, my name is _____ and I'd like to get to know you."

By Karl Fuchs

Kid Valentine Poems

I Like You

Valentine, I like you;
I'm glad that you're my friend;
We have lots of fun together,
We are a perfect blend!

By Joanna Fuchs

Fun to Be With

Please be my special Valentine;
There's no one quite like you.
You're really fun to be with,
And a very good friend, too!

By Joanna Fuchs

Give Me A Clue

I'm thinking of you on Valentine's Day;
You are nice, so I want to say:
Give me a clue; give me a sign;
Will you be my Valentine?

By Joanna Fuchs

Sunshine Valentine

I'll be very happy
If you'll be my Valentine;
You'll fill my heart with joy,
And my day with bright sunshine!

By Joanna Fuchs

When You're Around

Valentine, when you're around
My heart feels warm and happy.
I want to say 'I like you,"
Without sounding way too sappy!

By Joanna Fuchs

I Think You're Nice

I think you're nice; I think you're great.
You stand out from the rest.
And if you'll be my Valentine,
I'll think that you're the best!

By Joanna Fuchs

School Valentine

Valentine I see you
A lot when we're at school,
And every time I see you
I think you're very cool.

I'd like to know you better,
And so this poem I send,
Hoping that you'll soon be
My special Valentine friend.

By Joanna Fuchs

Valentine Blend

I think we make a perfect blend;
Will you be my Valentine friend?

By Joanna Fuchs

Fine Valentine

I like you; I think you're fine;
Will you be my Valentine?

By Joanna Fuchs

Valentine Treat

I hope your Valentine's Day is great.
I hope it's quite a treat.
I hope you have a happy day
Filled with things so sweet.

This poem's for you because I care.
I can't get more specific.
Well, yes I can, and here I go…
I think you're terrific!

By Joanna Fuchs

Mom Valentine

Mom, I've got some friends
Of each and every kind,
But a better friend than my mother
I'll never, ever find!

By Joanna Fuchs

Love You, Dad

Dad you are my favorite man,
And I sure want you to know,
I'll always respect and love you, Dad
No matter how big I grow!

By Joanna Fuchs

Special Grandma

Dear Grandma, you're so special
You do such nice things for me;
You love me just the way I am;
You make me happy as can be!

By Joanna Fuchs

Grandpa Contest

You are the greatest grandpa;
We have lots of fun.
If there were a grandpa contest,
You surely would have won!

By Joanna Fuchs

Brother Valentine

If I had to have a brother (ha, ha)
I'm glad it could be you.
I'm thankful to you, (name)
For the brotherly things you do!

By Joanna Fuchs

Sweet Sister

I'm glad to have a sister
Who is so nice and sweet.
As a good friend and a sister
My (name) can't be beat!

By Joanna Fuchs

Happy Family

I'm happy you're my (aunt, uncle, cousin, etc.)
I hope that you can see,
I'm really glad to have you as
A part of my family!

By Joanna Fuchs

Valentine Love Poems

A Joy I Never Knew

Have I told you, Valentine,
That I'm all wrapped up in you?
My feelings for you bring to me
A joy I never knew.

You light up everything for me;
In my heart you shine;
Illuminating my whole life,
My darling Valentine.

By Joanna Fuchs

Always Valentine

I'll always be the one who looks at you,
And sees you in a fond and loving light;
I'll always know that you're the one for me,
Because when we're together, life is right.

You'll always be my love--my hero, too,
The person I can count on constantly.
You satisfy me like no other could;
I'm ecstatic that it's you who makes us "we."

I'm always thankful for the day we met;
I love you, and I'm happy you are mine.
I'll always feel this joy, this bliss, this peace,
If you'll be my love forever, Valentine.

By Joanna Fuchs

Intoxicating Valentine

My Valentine, you're all I want;
In you, I find joy and delight;
You give me everything I need;
I'm happiest when you're in sight.

I think of you both night and day;
I'm drawn to you in pure attraction;
When you're not here, I ache for you,
For your fulfilling satisfaction.

I dreamed of love like this, and yet,
I never thought that I would capture
The deep, exciting thrills we have,
This intoxicating bliss and rapture.

Please be my Valentine, and more;
Be my life, my world, my all;
Together we can be content,
And share life's pleasures, big and small.

By Joanna Fuchs

Year Round Valentine

I love you all through February,
Not just on Valentine's Day;
I cherish you when flowers of spring
Appear in the midst of May.

I adore you in the summer,
When the air is filled with heat;
Without you in my life each day,
I wouldn't be complete.

I treasure you in fall,
When leaves are turning gold;
I loved you when you were younger;
I'll love you when you're old.

I prize you in the winter,
When colder days are here;
I love you, love you all the time,
Every minute of the year.

So I'll give to you this Valentine,
But I want to let you know,
It's not just today, but always,
That I will love you so.

By Joanna Fuchs

Will You Be My Valentine

My days are filled with yearning;
My nights are full of dreams.
I'm always thinking of you;
I'm in a trance, it seems.

You're all I ever wanted;
I wish you could be mine;
And so I have to ask you:
Will you be my Valentine?

By Joanna Fuchs

Forever Mine

My Valentine, I love just you;
My devotion I declare.
I'll spend my life looking for ways
To show you that I care.

Please say you feel the same for me;
Say you'll be forever mine;
We'll share a life of happiness,
My treasured Valentine.

By Joanna Fuchs

To My Friend, Lover and Partner on Valentine's Day

On Valentine's Day, I'm thinking of all the things you are
that make life more interesting and exciting, and blessed,
so much better in every way than it would be without you.
You're my friend...
You support me, encourage me, bring out the best in me.
I trust you and feel completely safe with you,
so I can share with you my hopes, my dreams,
and even secrets I've never told anyone else.
You've created a refuge for me to come to
when I need to escape from the hard edges of life.
You're my lover...
When we explore every part of each other,
touching, teasing,
creating ecstatic fever in each other,
such sweet torment--
I marvel that we can create together
such astonishing pleasure.
With you, I feel satisfied, complete,
wild and peaceful at the same time.
I've never felt this way with anyone else.
You're my partner...
You let me know that whatever life hands me
I'll have you on my side to help me.
I'm grateful for all that you give to me,
all that you do for me.
Together, we can live life to the fullest.
I'm so glad we found each other.
You're the joy of my life,
and I'm so very happy to have you as my Valentine!

By Joanna Fuchs

Why Do I Love You?

Why do I love you? I can't think of why,
Unless it's the sweet way that you make me sigh
With pleasure and rapture, emotion and bliss,
Each time that you hold me to give me a kiss.

Why do I love you? You've brought contentment and peace.
Each hour that I'm with you brings total release
From the cares of the day and the stresses of living.
You do that with caring and loving and giving.

Why do I love you? Reasons abound;
I know for a sure thing that I love the sound
Of your voice and your laugh, and I love your dear face,
And I know no one else could take your place.

Why do I love you? Did I mention your eyes?
The way that they smolder and hypnotize?
Your touch--what delicious sensations when we're...
Well...I'm crazy about you, I guess that's very clear.

May I be your sweetheart? And will you be mine?
Please say I can be your Valentine!

By Joanna Fuchs

I Don't Need Valentine's Day

I don't need Valentine's Day
to remember how much I love you,
or how much I want to give you
everything you need,
everything you want,
and delightful things
you haven't even thought of,
because you give so much to me.
I don't need Valentine's Day
to remind me to strive always
to create for you
surpassing happiness and satisfaction,
just as you have done for me.
I don't need Valentine's Day,
but it gives me a reason
to open my heart to you,

to tell you loving things
I think in my head
but forget to say out loud.
Happy Valentine's Day, Sweetheart;
You mean everything to me.

By Joanna Fuchs

Valentine Obsession

My Valentine, my love, my all,
How did this come to be?
This romance has me quite beguiled;
You've captivated me.

I breathe you every waking hour,
And when I sleep, I dream
That you are in my arms again...
Sweet fantasies extreme.

I'm sure that I was born for you;
You have me so fulfilled.
You kiss me and caress me,
As wild feelings start to build.

But that's not all, my Valentine;
My mind is also yours.
And for this fine obsession,
It seems there are no cures.

So tell me that you feel the same;
Tell me that you're mine.
Let me know you'll always be
My treasured Valentine.

By Joanna Fuchs

Every Day

Every day with you
is Valentine's Day, my love.
Every day is filled with romance,
love, with sharing and caring.
Every day I am reminded

how blessed I am to have you
as my Valentine, my sweetheart,
my lover, my friend,
my playmate, my companion.
No Valentine card,
no words at all could express
how much I love You,
how ecstatic I feel
to know that you are mine.
My Valentine,
every day, I'll try to show you
that every day I love you more.

By Joanna Fuchs

If I Could Write A Poem

I want to write a poem to tell you that I care,
And I'd write that poem to you, if only I would dare.
But poem writing scares me, so the outlook is quite bleak;
So to tell you of my feelings another outlet I must seek.

If I could write a poem, my problems would be solved;
I'd know exactly what to say; it wouldn't be involved.
I'd tell you of your grace, and of your wit and charm;.
I'd mention how your eyes shine and how your laugh disarms.

I'd tell you how I love you from your head down to your toe.
And you'd know it's all the truth because a poem told you so.
But I can't write a poem, so this note must break the ice,
And do the job to win your heart, nothing less will near suffice.

By Karl Fuchs

Is It You?

Valentine's Day will soon be here,
So I need to rush out and find,
A sweetheart to share that day with me,
It's driving me out of my mind.

Each year I let it slip away,
Next year will be time enough,

But next year comes and next year goes,
I'm still "I," not "We," and it's rough.

This seeking goes on day after day;
I keep looking for attributes fair.
My searching so far hasn't brought me success,
I can't stop though; I just wouldn't dare.

Somewhere there must be a sweetheart for me,
Someone attractive and true.
I hope that today this sweetheart I see...
Hey wait! Hello... Is it you?

By Karl Fuchs

WEDDING POEMS

The Best Is Yet To Be

On your joyful wedding day,
You begin a brand new life.
Friends and family give their gifts
To joyful husband, blissful wife.

But the greatest gift you'll ever get,
A gift from heaven above,
Is love forever, ending never,
Everlasting love.

You'll share life's joy and pleasure;
You'll have plenty of that, it's true.
But love is the real treasure
For your new spouse and you.

And if life hands you challenges,
As it does to one and all,
Your love will hold you steady
And never let you fall.

Your wedding day is full of joy;
Tomorrow you cannot see.
But one thing's sure for the two of you:
The best is yet to be.

By Joanna Fuchs

May All Good Things Be Yours

Your happiness begins
With your wonderful wedding day.
You'll share everything together;
Through it all, your love will stay.

Congratulations to you,
As you begin your happy life.

May all good things be yours,
As new husband and new wife.

By Joanna Fuchs

Marriage Glow

Your wedding day is just the start
Of a lifetime full of love and fun.
It just begins as you take your vows,
When the two of you are joined as one;

We wish for you sweet happiness;
Through the years, may your love grow,
To warm you both from day to day,
In your marriage's satisfying glow.

By Joanna Fuchs

The Finest Thing

Among the finest things in life,
a good marriage
is the most satisfying and rewarding,
the deepest and best of pleasures.
That blessed relationship
uplifts, enriches, encourages
and strengthens both husband and wife.
A loving marriage
overcomes any obstacles
the world may put in its way,
strengthening the special marital bond
with every challenge conquered.
Your wedding
is the start of something better
than you can imagine.
May your marriage
be all that you dream of and more.

By Joanna Fuchs

Door to Happiness

A wedding is a door to happiness,
When two decide to share their lives as one.
Your marriage is an adventure bright and new;
The pleasures and delights have just begun.

We wish for you a lifetime full of love;
May you always keep that magical attraction.
Let your bond and your commitment grow with time,
So that all your days are filled with satisfaction.

By Joanna Fuchs

Unshakeable Bond

A wedding of two people
of quality and character,
so obviously right for each other,
is a joy and a blessing to the world.
May your fondest hopes, wishes and dreams
all come true,
as you grow closer together
in an unshakeable, loving bond.
May your marriage be filled
with sunshine and rainbows
and every kind of happiness
you two so richly deserve.
Congratulations, and every good wish
for the best things life has to offer you.

By Joanna Fuchs

Wonderful Life

Congratulations on your marriage,
Have a wonderful life!
You are two terrific people,
Now teamed as man and wife.

A team with blessings like yours
Will live a life you'll cherish;

You'll find happiness everywhere,
For your love will never perish.

By Karl Fuchs

Wedding Invitation Poem

You're Invited!

A wedding is coming!
Details inside.
Come celebrate
With the groom and the bride.

There'll be music and food,
Joy and fun—come and see,
And please let us know
With your RSVP.

By Joanna Fuchs

Wedding Program or Thank You Poem

The Rest Of Our Life

Today we begin the rest of our life
Together forever as husband and wife.
Our dreams came true, with love and more—
Adventures to have and the world to explore.

We'll share our joys, we'll share our sorrows;
We can already see many bright tomorrows.
We'll share our friends and family, too,
And you are part of that special crew.

Thank you for celebrating our wedding day.
As we share our vows, we just want to say:
These wedding memories will become a treasure,
And seeing you here is part of the pleasure.

By Joanna Fuchs

May All Your Dreams Come True

Here's to Jim and Kathy:
May they always love each other as much as they do today.
Now each of you has a best friend forever.
Each of you is a shelter for the other from life's storms.
Each of you can share with each other life's greatest pleasures.
This is a great beginning, but the best is yet to come.
Let today's treasured memories turn into beautiful tomorrows
full of joy, fun, contentment and satisfaction.
The world always welcomes lovers,
and the whole wide world is opening up for you now
to share its treasures and delights.
May all your dreams come true, and may we get to share in them!

By Joanna Fuchs

Perfect Partner

Here's to Brad and Jill:
May they find in each other
the perfect partner for life's adventure.
May their marriage be filled with happiness
exceeding their wildest dreams.
May they see again each and every day
all the qualities in the other
that made them fall in love and marry.
And may they always be grateful
for life's greatest gift--
a marriage based on true love.
May your true love give both of you
joy, and peace, and satisfaction.

By Joanna Fuchs

Wedding Vows

Bride's Vow

My wonderful (groom's name),
On our wedding day, I think of all the reasons
I am blessed to be your wife:

You are the joy of my life.
In you I found much more than I ever hoped,
more than I ever dreamed a man could be.
In your arms, I feel happy, safe, protected.
You're my hero, my defender, my soul mate, my love.

I was born for you.
There was a space in my heart that you fill perfectly.
I fall in love with you again every time I see you.

We are alike, and yet we are different.
Our similarities bond us together,
and our differences keep things interesting.
And no matter what,
you let me be me, just as I am.
I am so grateful for that.

I want to keep discovering you.
I love so many things about you now,
and I know I will find many more to love.

The many little things you to do please me
touch me more than you know.
You see me with your heart,
and you always make me feel beautiful.

This is the beginning
of the rest of our lives together.
We have so much happiness ahead of us,
a lifetime of love,
a lifetime to create wonderful memories.
Nothing matters more than being with you.
I love you; I trust you; I am totally open to you.

Everything that's woman in me responds to the man in you,
And as we become husband and wife,

I want you to know that there will never be
anyone else for me but you,
my husband, my love, my life.

By Joanna Fuchs

Groom's Vow

My sweet (bride's name)
On our wedding day, I think of all the reasons
I am blessed to be your husband:

You are the joy of my life.
You are everything I ever wanted in a woman.
My heart soars every time I see you.
Just the sound of your voice brings me pleasure.
I never get enough of you.

When I'm with you I feel happy, complete, confident, strong,
everything a man wants to feel.
You're the best thing that ever happened to me.

I'm a better person when I'm around you.
You bring out good parts of me I didn't even know I had.
You inspire me to be the best I can be.
I'm better for knowing you, better for loving you.

You're so easy to love.
You brighten my life in so many ways.
When you're not with me, I miss you.
It feels like we were meant for each other.
It means so much to me to have you by my side.

I can't find words to say
how intense my feelings are for you.
You thrill me beyond description.
I didn't know what happiness was till I met you.

You're my serenity, my comforter,
a peaceful refuge from the outside world.
No one else knows me like you do.
I share things with you I've never shared before,
and you use the things you discover about me
to do things that make me happy.

I am so grateful for that.
I love you; I trust you; I am totally open to you.

Everything that's man in me
responds to the woman in you
And as we become husband and wife,
There will never be anyone else for me,
My wife, my love, my life.

By Joanna Fuchs

More Vows

(Man's name), I've dreamed of the man I'd want to be with forever: strong, smart, kind, tender, romantic. You're better than I dreamed. When I'm with you, my heart glows with pleasure, and I wonder how I could be so blessed. I was born for you. Let me be your friend, your playmate, your biggest fan. I offer you my heart, my mind, my life.

(Woman's name), I always knew the kind of woman I wanted: bright, attractive, fun-loving, affectionate. You're all that and more. When we're together, I'm happier than I've ever been before. You bring out the best in me. You're so easy to love, and no one can love you like I do. Let me be your hero, your lover, your greatest admirer. I offer you myself, my love, my life.

By Joanna Fuchs

MISCELLANEOUS RHYMING POEMS

Spring Poem

Sweet Spring

When the gloomy gray sky turns to clear azure blue,
And the snow disappears from the ground,
When the birds start to sing, and our moods start to lift,
Then we know Spring is coming around.

When the first flower bulbs poke their heads toward the sun,
Golden daffodils, hyacinths, too;
When the brown grass turns green, and the wildflowers bloom,
Then sweet Spring makes its showy debut.

Once again we awake from cold winter's pale dream,
As our minds and our bodies revive;
We rejoice and delight in spring's colorful sight;
Each new spring makes us glad we're alive!

By Joanna Fuchs

Summer Poems

Summer Pleasures

Sunshine beaming golden heat
For lots of fun outdoors;
Vacations, for a sweet retreat
To mountains, plains and shores.

Kids in constant summer motion,
Free from teacher's rule,
Head to toe in suntan lotion,
At the beach or pool.

Inflatable rafts on which to float,
Camping and fishing gear,
Rowing or sailing or water-ski boat,
Tell us summer's here.

Things we can't do the rest of the year
Are summer's special treasures;
Oh summer, summer, linger long,
And give us all your pleasures!

By Joanna Fuchs

Summer Delights

Healing summer heat
That comforts every bone;
Juicy summer fruits,
A frosty ice cream cone.

Aroma of sizzling meat
Grilling on the barbecue,
Green lawns and summer flowers,
A gazillion fun things to do.

Summer shorts and swimsuits,
Arms and legs are bare;
Summer's sweet delights
Are welcome everywhere!

By Joanna Fuchs

Fall Poems
––––––––––––––

Flamboyant Autumn

Autumn's picturesque arrival
Is a colorful array
Of red and gold and orange,
In flamboyant, rich display.

Autumn days are shorter;
The nights are getting cool;
Geese fly south in flocks,
As kids go back to school.

Winter still is dreaming
Of snow and icicles,

As we put away our swimsuits,
Our boats and bicycles.

Wisps of smoke from chimneys
Tell of cozy, crackling fires;
Fall is being born,
As summer now retires.

By Joanna Fuchs

Fall's Chores

Summer's getting drowsy now;
Soon she will be dozing;
Flowers are folding up their heads,
Another season's closing.

Fall is waiting in the wings,
Impatient to get going,
He has a lot of work to do,
Before it's time for snowing.

"I have to paint the leaves," he says,
"In shades of red and gold,
And send the geese along their way
Before it gets too cold.

"I'll ripen pumpkins on the vine,
For sweet Thanksgiving pies,
And plump the apples on the trees
To make cider that satisfies.

"Sunshiny days will be shorter now;
I'll add a cool, crisp breeze;
For this relief from summer heat,
I make no apologies.

"I have just one more thing to do;
My work is almost done;
I'll turn the leaves to crunchy piles,
So kids can have fall fun!"

By Joanna Fuchs

Fall Ballet

In fall the leaves are dancing
In the newly cool, crisp breeze,
Tumbling, skipping, flipping,
As they throw themselves from trees.

Twirling, whirling dancers,
Give performances each day,
Floating gracefully to earth,
In a circular ballet.

And as they land together,
Making not a sound,
They form a comfy quilt,
For the cooling winter ground.

By Joanna Fuchs

Winter Poem

Winter's Embrace

When winter blows its cold breath everywhere,
And throws a chill white blanket on the ground,
The sun makes sparkling diamonds on the snow,
And trees with icy diadems are crowned.

It's time to snuggle in for winter fun
In cozy places, maybe by a fire.
A good book and some cocoa feel just right
In flannels, sweaters, winter's warm attire.

Winter's gloom is comforting somehow,
As life retreats from its rushed and frantic pace.
We're ready now to stay indoors awhile,
As we settle into winter's calm embrace.

By Joanna Fuchs

Miss You Poem

I Miss You

I miss you in the morning;
I miss you late at night.
Just to think about you
Is my joy and my delight.

I can't wait to see you;
Please hurry and come back.
You always make me happy;
You have that special knack!

By Joanna Fuchs

Retirement Poem

Good Memories

Your retirement leaves a great big gap
In all our lives and hearts;
A workplace is never quite the same
When someone like you departs.

You've enriched us in so many ways;
We'll miss you more than you know;
We wish you luck, and hope you take
Good memories when you go.

By Joanna Fuchs

Thinking of You Poem

Remembering Times

I'm thinking of you
With joy and pleasure,
Remembering times
I'll always treasure.

When I think of you,
My heart is light;
You're a special person,
A sheer delight.

Thoughts of you cheer me up
Whenever I'm blue;
I'm always happy
When I think of you.

I think of you often,
In the fondest way;
I cherish you more
Than I ever could say.

By Joanna Fuchs

Inspirational and Life Poems

We Don't Know Why

The twinkling of stars on a balmy night,
The gabble of geese as they take flight,
A passionate look in your lover's eye,
The graceful ballet of a butterfly.

Living on the edge, in a committed way,
Facing all challenges day by day,
Your life on the line—to do, not just try,
Life is exciting—a natural high.

Failure and boredom appear in your life;
Unhappiness cuts you, just like a knife.
"Where are all the good times," you cry;
Is life just hard, and then you die?"

The freshening feel of an ocean breeze,
The colors of change in the leaves on the trees,
The feeling of peace as the days go by,
Life's a dazzling puzzle—and we don't know why.

By Karl and Joanna Fuchs

Find Your Thankful Self

Sometimes you feel you're nothing at all,
And that's all you'll ever be.
You study all your defects;
An empty life is all you see.

Instead of looking at what you haven't got,
Seeing only what you lack,
Focus on your blessings,
And get right back on track.

There are many good things about being you;
Count them one by one.
Your life has lots of comforts,
While others, they have none.

Many people have it much, much worse
Yet they have happiness.
They take joy in little things
They're thankful, though they have less.

Lift your spirits up right now;
Get out of that depression.
Find your thankful self,
And give it full expression.

Find the joy in little things;
Focus on fun and laughter.
See life's blessings all around,
And live happily ever after!

By Joanna Fuchs

Forgiveness or Apology Poem

Please Forgive Me

When I said what I said, I was wrong;
Please forgive me, and let's start anew.
Our relationship means much to me.
I'm so sorry my blunder hurt you.

Though your memory may bring it back up,
Won't you please try to put it away?
I'll be tactful and sensitive now;
I'll think of your needs every day.

Let's go on with our lives as we were;
I'd take it all back if I could.
Let's focus on positive things;
What we have is important and good.

By Joanna Fuchs